Give instructions
**Spanish**

(an English/Spanish pocket guide)


**Spanish for Radiology Professionals** contains English to Spanish translations of often-used, technical terms and Radiological instructions. Chapters are categorized with prone and supine instructions as in CT scans, MRI and Ultrasound, plus specific instructions for Mammography and General x-ray studies. Easy to use, even for someone with limited Spanish.


Examples of entries: (The Spanish includes a phonetic spelling guide for easy pronunciation)


*Can you...stand up?*   ¿*Puede usted...pararse?*

  *PWEH-deh oosTED ...pahRAHR-seh*

*...open your mouth?*   *...abra la boca?*

  *AH-brah lah BOH-kah*

*Take off...your shoes.*   *Quítese... los zapatos.*

  *KEEteh-seh... los sah-PAHtos*

**Peltrovijan Publishing**
**P.O. Box 13**
**Shrub Oak NY 10588**
**http://www.opeart.com**

The author does not guarantee and assumes no responsibility on the accuracy of any websites, links or other contacts contained in this book.

Spanish for Radiology Professionals:

An English/Spanish Pocket Guide

3rd Edition

All rights reserved.

Copyright © 2018

Peltrovijan Publishing / published by arrangement with the author

Printing History

1997/2010

Cover design and digital illustration

By Nadine Peart Akindele, MD

No part of this book may be used or reproduced by any means, graphic, electronic, or mechanical, including scanning, photocopying, recording, taping or by any information storage retrieval system without the written permission of the publisher except in the case of brief quotations embodied in critical articles and reviews. Please do not encourage piracy or plagiarization of copyrighted material in violation of the author's rights. Purchase only authorized editions.

ISBN-13: 978-1-937143-46-6

Printed in the United States of America

# ACKNOWLEDGMENTS

As with any book, the help of others is often invaluable. I would like to give special thanks to my family for their understanding and support.

Special thanks to Angelic Pla and Nadine Peart for their enthusiastic help.

Thanks also to Edwin Resto and Lizette Padilla. Without their help the first edition would not exist.

# Also by Olive Peart

**Mind Games**
Matthew has the uncanny ability to influence people's thought. To defend himself against the bullies, Matthew is eventually forced to use his special power.
ISBN: 978 976 638 167 7

**The Starlight Kids, Mystery of the Feather Burglar**
With the help of her friends, Shari gets her chance to turn a boring summer vacation into a fantastic action packed adventure.
ISBN 13 Print: 978-0-9845497-5-7     ISBN 13 eBook: 978-0-9845497-6-4
Audio Book ISBN: 978-0-9823077-7-9

**The Intruders– In This War They Had The Advantage**
Six Bronx teens have one thing in common–a thirst for excitement! They get that and more when they set out to explore a neglected track of land in their neighborhood and embark on an adventure of a lifetime. Unfortunately, within weeks, their adventure becomes all too real as brother turns against brother, friends become enemies and people are being killed! This is no longer fun. This is war!
ISBN-13: 978-0-9845497-7-1     ISBN-13 eBook: 978-0-9845497-4-0
ISBN Audio: 978-0-9823077-6-2

**Linked**
Same age, same height, same grade—they could have been identical twins, but they were not. Yet they lived in the same imperfect world with overwhelming family problems... One was black and the other was white and they had switched!
ISBN-13: 978-0-9823077-0-0     ISBN eBook: 978-0-9823077-1-7

**Life After High School: Traits that Help and Traits that Hurt**
This no-nonsense text explains positive and negative traits that can help or hinder teens in their post high school life. The guide gives readers strategies, helping them to identify the path to success and to avoid the route that often leads to failure.
ISBN-13: 978-1-937143-14-5     ISBN -13: eBook 978-1-937143-15-2

**The Dangers of Medical Radiation**
It is one of the ironies of medicine that radiation, as in x-rays, CT scans, radiation therapy and nuclear medicine can cause cancer yet can be used to detect and treat cancer. Perhaps because of this irony, most of us know very little about radiation dangers. Read how to protect yourself from medical radiation!
ISBN-13: 978-0-9829774-1-5     ISBN -13: eBook 978-0-9829774-2-2

# BOOKS FOR IMAGING PROFESSIONALS

**Lange Radiographic Positioning Flashcards (Lange).**
**1st Edition.** ISBN: 9780071797320
A comprehensive, carry-anywhere review of routine imaging procedures, projections, and positioning terminology. Included all the ARRT competency required projections.
Great for use as a radiography procedures course review or as a clinical refresher prior to taking a patient's x-ray.

**Mammography & Breast Imaging Prep. Program Review. 2nd Edition.** ISBN: 9781259859458
1st ed. ISBN-13: 978-0071749329
A comprehensive review for the mammography ARRT registry examination including the history of breast imaging, breast cancer detection, and treatment (including new imaging methods and recent advances in digital mammography, MRI, BSGI, DBT, volumtetric ultrasound imaging, and Cone Beam Breast CT)

**Lange Q & A Mammography Examination. 4th ed.**
ISBN: 9781259859434
3rd ed. ISBN-13: 978-0071833929;
2ndEdition-ISBN-13: 9780071548359
Everything you need to ace the ARRT Mammography Exam in one complete study package! This comprehensive study guide for the ARRT's Mammography Examination summarizes the mammography curriculum in a concise, readable format and includes 450 ARRT-style questions plus two complete practice exams to give radiographic technicians the practice they need to pass the registry examination with flying colors.

**Mammography and Breast Imaging: Just the Facts.**
**1st Edition.** ISBN-13: 9780071431200
The perfect review tool for radiologic technologists certifying or recertifying. Following the guidelines specified by the American Registry of Radiologic Technologist (ARRT) Exam, the book includes all breast imaging modalities and techniques as well as questions for self-assessment.

AN ENGLISH/SPANISH POCKET GUIDE

# SPANISH FOR RADIOLOGY PROFESSIONALS

3RD EDITION

# OLIVE PEART

*PELTROVIJAN PUBLISHING*

*Olive loves to hear from her readers.
Visit her at www.opeart.com*

# Table of Content

| | |
|---|---:|
| *HOW TO BEST UTILIZE THIS BOOK* | *11* |
| *SPANISH PRONUNCIATION* | *13* |
|   *SPANISH VOWELS* | *13* |
| *SPANISH GRAMMAR IN BRIEF* | *14* |
|   *NOUNS* | *14* |
|   *ARTICLES* | *14* |
|   *PRONOUNS* | *15* |
|     *Personal Pronouns* | *15* |
|     *Direct Object Pronouns* | *15* |
|     *Indirect Object Pronouns* | *16* |
|     *Possessive Pronouns* | *16* |
|     *Reflexive Pronouns* | *16* |
|     *Demonstrative Pronouns* | *17* |
|   *ADJECTIVES* | *17* |
|     *Demonstrative Adjectives* | *17* |
|     *Possessive Adjectives* | *17* |
|   *COMPARATIVE AND SUPERLATIVE* | *18* |
|   *ADVERBS* | *19* |
|   *-ING ENDINGS* | *19* |
|   *POSSESSION* | *19* |
|   *DIRECT COMMANDS* | *19* |
|   *VERBS* | *20* |
|     *Regular verbs* | *20* |
|     *Reflexive Verbs* | *20* |
|     *Irregular Verbs* | *20* |
|   *SAME SPELLING/DIFFERENT MEANINGS* | *21* |
|   *PUNCTUATION MARKS* | *21* |
| *REFERENCE* | *22* |
|   *NUMBERS* | *22* |
|     *Cardinal Numbers* | *22* |
|     *Ordinal Numbers* | *23* |
|     *Fractions* | *24* |
|     *Number Phrases* | *24* |
|   *TEMPERATURE* | *24* |
|   *MONTHS* | *24* |
|   *SEASONS* | *25* |
|   *FAMILY* | *25* |
|   *PEOPLE* | *26* |
|   *DAYS OF THE WEEK* | *26* |
|   *TIME* | *26* |
|   *DAYS AND DATES* | *29* |

| | |
|---|---:|
| COLOR AND CLOTHING | 32 |
|    *Color* | 32 |
|    *Clothing* | 32 |
| BONES & BODY PARTS | 34 |
| GENERAL GREETINGS | 37 |
|    USEFUL QUESTIONS AND EXPRESSIONS | 39 |
| UNDERSTANDING YOUR PATIENT | 48 |
|    GENERAL QUESTIONS AND EXPRESSIONS | 48 |
|    POSSIBLE ANSWERS OR DIRECTIONS | 55 |
| PROBLEMS AND EMERGENCIES | 58 |
|    GENERAL QUESTIONS AND EXPRESSIONS | 58 |
|    RELATED QUESTIONS AND REPLIES | 63 |
| FILLING OUT FORMS | 67 |
|    GENERAL QUESTIONS AND EXPRESSIONS | 67 |
|    RELATED REPLIES | 70 |
| PATIENT CARE | 71 |
|    GENERAL QUESTIONS | 71 |
|    POSSIBLE RESPONSES | 77 |
| UNDRESSING THE PATIENT | 79 |
| ULTRASOUND / RECUMBENT EXAMINATIONS | 82 |
| ERECT EXAMINATIONS | 85 |
|    OTHER NECESSARY INSTRUCTIONS | 89 |
|    POSSIBLE RESPONSES | 91 |
| PATIENT EVALUATION | 92 |
|    GENERAL | 92 |
|    POSSIBLE RESPONSES | 99 |
| FEMALE EVALUATION | 100 |
|    POSSIBLE RESPONSE | 101 |
| PREPARATION STUDIES | 102 |
|    GIVING AN INTRAVENOUS | 102 |
|    POSSIBLE RESPONSES | 103 |
| CONTRAST STUDIES | 104 |
|    ENEMAS | 106 |
|    POSSIBLE RESPONSES | 109 |
| MAMMOGRAM EXAMS | 110 |
|    GENERAL QUESTIONS AND EXPRESSIONS | 110 |
|    POSSIBLE RESPONSES | 114 |
| MRI EXAMINATIONS | 115 |
|    GENERAL QUESTIONS | 115 |
| ADDRESSING THE PARENT/GUARDIAN | 119 |
| ENGLISH-SPANISH DICTIONARY | 121 |
|    *Author's Bio* | 165 |

# HOW TO BEST UTILIZE THIS BOOK

This book was not designed to teach the Spanish language. However, Spanish for Radiology Professionals-3rd edition can easily be used by someone with a limited knowledge of Spanish.

The main purpose of the book is to communicate your instructions to the patient and to understand everyday emergency situations the Spanish patient may present.

The emphasis is on being understood and not necessarily on achieving an authentic Spanish accent. Most of the Spanish used is followed by a phonetic transcription, syllable by syllable, showing you how to pronounce the words. The upper-case letters in the transcription indicate the stressed syllables. The transcription is based on the common pronunciations, and should be read just as one would read ordinary English. Please also note that although the transcription is divided into syllables, spoken Spanish is a fast and fluid language. The stressed syllables should be pronounced louder but try to keep the stressed and unstressed syllables the same length, pronouncing each group of syllables as one word.

The Spanish in this book translates simple everyday phrases technologists use in radiologic departments of hospitals, health care centers and clinics. Most of the phrases and expressions are simple and easy to remember. The Spanish translations can enable you to provide patient care to your Spanish patients and help the Spanish patient who is seeking information or directions.

While it is not necessary to memorize the entire book, if you are really interested in learning to communicate with your patients, it's essential that you at least read through the reference chapters to obtain a basic knowledge of the Spanish language, practice your pronunciations and familiarize yourself with the grammar. A review of the entire book you would then be able to pick out a few useful phrases to memorize. After that, the book can be kept in your pocket as a quick reference when needed.

Any comments, criticism and suggestions that you think may be of help in preparing future editions will be gratefully appreciated. Please contact me by visiting my web site www.opeart.com.

Olive Peart, M.S.,R.T.(R)(M))

# SPANISH PRONUNCIATION

## SPANISH VOWELS
There are 5 distinct vowels in Spanish

| | | |
|---|---|---|
| a | ah | -a- as in APPLE |
| e | eh | -e- as in MET |
| i | ee | -ee- as in BEE |
| o | oh | -o- as in NO |
| u | oo | -oo- as in BOOT |

Many of the consonants are very similar to the English.

| | | |
|---|---|---|
| b | beh | similar to the English -b- as in BOOK |
| c | seh | before an -e- or -i- pronounced -s- as in SO otherwise it is pronounced -k- as in KING |
| ch | chay | similar to -ch- as in CHURCH |
| d | dey | similar to the English -d- as in DOG |
| f | eh-fey | similar to the English -f- as in FAST |
| g | gey | if followed by-a-,-o- or -u- the -g- sounds -g- as in GO Before -a-, -e- or -i- the -g- is like and -h- as in HIT |
| h | ah-chey | the -h- in Spanish is never pronounced |
| j | hota | always pronounced as -h- as in HOT |
| k | kah | similar to the English -c- as in SCATTER |
| l | eh-ley | similar to the English -l- as in LOVE |
| ll | ey-yey | pronounced -y- as in YES. In some places it can sound similar to the -ll- in MILLION. |
| m | eh-mey | similar to the English -m- |
| n | eh-ney | similar to the English -n- as in NICE |
| ñ | eh-nyeh | pronounced as -ny- as in CANYON |
| p | peh | similar to the English -p- as in SPOT |
| q | coo | always followed by the -u- and pronounced -k- as in KING If -qu- is also followed by -e- or -i- the -u- is silent. |
| r | eh-rey | pronounced like the letter -d- or -tt- as in LITTLE |
| rr | erh-rey | the -rr- sound is not used in the English language. It is pronounced as a trill sound |
| s | eh-sey | similar to the English -s- as in SEE. If followed by a constant is sound like the -z- |
| t | teh | similar to the English -t- as in STOP |
| v | beh | similar to the -b- as in BOOK |
| w | doble beh | never used in Spanish |
| x | eh-kees | similar to the English -s- if at the beginning of a word or sound like a -x- as in EXIT |
| y | ee-greh-gah | pronounced -j- as in JOY by itself or in front of a vowel pronounced-ee- as BEE |
| z | seh-tah | pronounced -s- as in SO or in some regions -th- as in THIN |

Also remember:
- In Spanish the next-to-last syllable of words ending in a vowel, -n or -s is always stressed.
- The last syllable of words ending in a consonant (except the -n or -s ) is stressed.
- All words that do not follow these rules have a written accent.

# SPANISH GRAMMAR IN BRIEF

## NOUNS

All nouns in Spanish are either masculine or feminine.

Masculine nouns generally end with -o- or are names that are naturally masculine.
e.g. el hombre            the man.

Days of the week, months, rivers, oceans, and mountains are also masculine.

Feminine nouns generally end with -a- and are also nouns that are naturally feminine.
e.g. la mujer             the woman.

–The two exceptions are "la mano," hand and "el día," day.

In most cases to change a word from masculine to feminine simply change the ending of the word from -o- to -a-.
e.g. el niño    the boy    &    la niña    the girl

For masculine nouns ending in -ón-, -or- and -án-, add an -a- for the feminine.
e.g. el doctor            la doctora


## ARTICLES

The articles in Spanish agree with the nouns in gender and number.
The definite articles -the- are: el, la, los, las.
The indefinite articles -a-, -an-, -some-, -one- are: un, una, unos, unas.

|      |             | **Singular**  |                  | **Plural**  |
|------|-------------|---------------|------------------|-------------|
| mas. | the/a boy   | el/un niño    | the boys         | los niños   |
|      |             |               | boys/some boys   | unos niños  |
| fem. | the/a girl  | la/una niña   | the girls        | las niñas   |
|      |             |               | girls/some girls | unas niñas  |

Definite articles are used instead of possessive adjectives for objects close to the body and for body parts.
e.g. levante las manos       lift your hands

# PRONOUNS

## Personal Pronouns

| | |
|---|---|
| I | yo |
| you | tú—used to address close relatives friends or children |
| you | usted—the polite form used to address strangers    * |
| he/she/it | él/ella |
| we | nosotros/nosotras |
| you(pl.) | ustedes—polite form |
| they | ellos/ellas |

Pronouns in front of the verb are frequently omitted in Spanish except in the polite form (usted, ustedes ).
e.g. Yo hablo español.    –becomes–    Hablo español.
   I speak Spanish

If a group contains even one male, the masculine form of the pronoun is used.
e.g. When referring to all females:
   Nosotras estamos en la sala de rayos X.    We're in the x-ray room.
   Ellas están en la sala de rayos X    They are in the x-ray room.

   When speaking about a mixed group:
   Nosotros estamos en la sala de rayos X    We're in the x-ray room.
   Ellos están en la sala de rayos X    They are in the x-ray room.

* usted is often abreviated -ud-

## Direct Object Pronouns

Direct object pronouns are used instead of direct objects.

| | |
|---|---|
| me | me |
| you | te |
| you | lo (polite form) |
| him/her/it | lo/la |
| us | nos |
| you(pl.) | los (polite form) |
| them | los/las |

Direct object pronouns are placed before a conjugated verb.
e.g. ¿Dónde le duele?    Where does it hurt?

## Indirect Object Pronouns

An indirect object usually tells to whom or for whom something is done.

| | |
|---|---|
| to me | me |
| to you | te |
| to you | le (polite form) |
| to him/her | le |
| to us | nos |
| to you(pl.) | les (polite form) |
| to them | les |

The indirect object pronoun is usually placed in front of the verb. When used with an infinitive, it can be attached to the infinitive, forming one word.
e.g. ¿En qué puedo ayudarle?  Can I help you?

## Possessive Pronouns

Possessive pronouns agree in gender and number with the person or thing possessed and are generally used with the definite articles. (el, la, los & las)

The exception is with the verb -ser-: to be.
e.g. Son mías. -not- Son las mías.  They are mine.

| | Singular | | Plural | |
|---|---|---|---|---|
| | Mas.(el) | Fem.(la) | Mas.(los) | Fem.(las) |
| mine | mío | mía | míos | mías |
| yours | tuyo | tuya | tuyos | tuyas |
| yours (*polite form*) suyo his/hers | | suya | suyos | suyas |
| ours | nuestro | nuestra | nuestros | nuetras |
| theirs | suyo | suya | suyos | suyas |

## Reflexive Pronouns

In Spanish the reflexive pronoun is often understood but not used. If used the reflexive pronouns are placed before the verb in the sentence.
e.g. El paciente se viste:   The patient dresses himself.

| | subject | reflex.pronoun |
|---|---|---|
| myself, to(for)myself | yo | me |
| yourself, to(for) yourself | tú | te |
| yourself, to(for) yourself himself, herself, itself | usted | se |
| to(for) himself, herself, itself | él/ella | se |
| ourselves, to(for) ourselves | nosotros | nos |
| yourselves, to(for)yourselves (formal) | ustedes | se |
| themselves, to(for) themselves | ellos/ellas | se |

## Demonstrative Pronouns

The neuter pronouns can be used to refer to situations or ideas.
All the demonstrative pronouns have a written accent to differentiate them from the demonstrative adjectives. The exceptions are the neuter pronouns. They have no accent marks because there are no corresponding demonstrative adjectives.

|  | Mas. | Fem. | Neuter |
|---|---|---|---|
| this | éste | ésta | esto |
| these | éstos | éstas | estos |
| that | ése | ésa | eso |
| those | ésos | ésas | esos |
| that(one) | aquél | aquélla | aquello |
| those (at a distance) | aquéllos | aquéllas | aquellos |

# ADJECTIVES

## Demonstrative Adjectives

Demonstrative adjectives point out persons and things. They agree in gender and number with the nouns they modify and are placed after the noun. The forms of the demonstrative adjectives are the same as those of the demonstrative pronouns except that the demonstrative adjectives do not have a written accent.

Spanish adjectives can therefore have four forms, depending on whether the nouns they describe are masculine or feminine, singular or plural.

## Possessive Adjectives

Possessive adjectives agree in number with the nouns they modify.(That is, what is possessed).

|  | Sing. | Plur. |
|---|---|---|
| my | mi | mis |
| your | tu | tus |
| your(polite) | su | sus |
| his/hers/it | su | sus |
| our | nuestro/a | nuestros/as |
| their | su | sus |

Nuestros is the only possessive adjective that agrees in number AND IN GENDER with what is possessed.

| e.g. | nuestro hijo | our son |
|---|---|---|
|  | nuestra hija | our daughter |
|  | nuestros hijos | our sons |
|  | nuestras hijas | our daughters |

In general adjectives in Spanish agree in gender and number with the noun. Qualifying adjectives ( good, color, etc.) generally follow nouns, while adjectives of quantity ( four, many, etc. ) precede them.

e.g. el libro azul      the blue book
    los libros azules      the blue books
    cuatro libros      four books

- Adjectives ending in -o- change to -a- for the feminine form. The following words all mean exactly the same thing (tall)

| Singular | Plural | |
|---|---|---|
| e.g. alto | altos | tall |
| chico alto | chicos altos | tall boys |
| chica alta | chicas altas | tall girls |

**This is true for all adjectives whose base form ends in –o-,-or-, -n-, -on- or -ín-**

Adjectives ending in -e- or a consonant have the same masculine and feminine forms. These adjectives only change for singular and plural (not masculine or feminine).

e.g. chico inteligente      chicos inteligentes      intelligent boy/s
    chica inteligente      chicas inteligentes      intelligent girl/s

The exception to this is any adjective of nationality ending in a consonant in which case an -a- is added in the feminine.

e.g. el niño español      the Spanish boy
    la niña española      the Spanish girl

# COMPARATIVE AND SUPERLATIVE

In Spanish, apart from a few irregular forms, the comparative is formed by adding -más que- (more than) or -menos que- (less than) before the adjective or adverb.

e.g. La enfermera es más alta que tu.      The nurse is taller than you.

Superlatives are formed by placing the definite article (el or la) before the person or thing being compared.

e.g. La enfermera más alta.      The tallest nurse.

# ADVERBS

Adverbs which are formed in the English language by adding -ly- to the adjective form of the word, are formed in the Spanish language by adding -mente- to the feminine form of the adjective. For adjectives ending in -o- change the -o- to -a- before adding -mente.
e.g. lento:slow              lentamente:slowly
     rápido:rapid            rápidamente:rapidly

If two or more adjectives are used together change the -o- to -a- in both but end only the last one with -mente.
e.g. slowly and carefully     lenta y cuidadosamente

# -ING ENDINGS

The verbal endings -ando- and -iendo- translate to the English ending -ing. In Spanish the verb "to be" -estar- is used with the past participle.
e.g. Estoy escribiendo       I am writing
     ¿Está usted usando...?    Are you wearing...?

# POSSESSION

Instead of the apostrophe Spanish uses the word -de- or -del- (literally a contraction of de + el).
e.g. La requisición del paciente      The patient's requisition
     La radiografía de la niña        The girl's x-ray

# DIRECT COMMANDS

When giving a direct affirmative command, the object pronouns are placed after the verb and are attached to it, forming one word. In the negative command the object pronouns are placed in front of the verb.
e.g. ¡Escribalo aquí!        Write that down here!
     ¡No los ponga aquí!     Do not put them here!

Note that negatives in Spanish are formed simply by putting -no- in front of the verb.
e.g. ¡No toque aqui!         Do not touch here!

# VERBS

## Regular verbs

There are three main categories of regular verbs in Spanish: those ending in either -ar, -er or -ir.

- For -ar verbs, drop the ending and add o, a, amos, an.
- For -er verbs, drop the ending and add o, e, emos, en.
- For -ir verbs, drop the ending and add o, e, imos, en.

**e.g. comer - to eat**

| | | | |
|---|---|---|---|
| I eat | yo como | we eat(m) | nosotros comemos |
| | | we eat (f) | nosotras comemos |
| you eat | usted come | you eat (pl) | ustedes comen |
| he/it eats | él come | they eat (m/pl) | ellos comen |
| she/it eats | ella come | they eat (f/pl) | ellas comen |

**e.g. vivir - to live**

| | | | |
|---|---|---|---|
| I live | yo vivo | we live (m) | nosotros vivimos |
| | | we live (f) | nosotras vivimos |
| you live | usted vive | you live (pl) | ustedes viven |
| he/it lives | él vive | they live (m/pl) | ellos viven |
| she/it live | ella vive | they live (f/pl) | llas viven |

## Reflexive Verbs

Most verbs can be made reflexive in Spanish by adding the reflexive pronoun. Reflexive verbs act upon the subject.

## Irregular Verbs

Below are the conjugations in the present tense of the verbs -ser- & -estar.- Both ser and estar mean "to be."

- Ser- used to describe a permanent conditions such as time, dates, occupation and relationships
- Estar- used to describe a temporary conditions such as location, state, condition and progressive tenses.

| | | SER | ESTAR |
|---|---|---|---|
| I am | yo | soy | estoy |
| you are | usted | es | está |
| her/she/it is | el(ella) | es | está |
| we are | nosotros/as | somos | estamos |
| you are | ustedes | son | están |
| they are | ellos(ellas) | son | están |

Other Spanish verbs are irregular verbs and their conjugations have to be learned.

# SAME SPELLING/DIFFERENT MEANINGS

Words that have the same spelling but different meanings

| | | | |
|---|---|---|---|
| el | the | él | he, him |
| mas | but | más | more |
| mi | my | mí | me |
| si | if | sí | yes |
| te | you | té | tea |
| tu | your | tú | you |

**Also:**  éste  this

With the accent it is used as a pronoun, but without the accent it is an adjective or it can be a noun.
e.g. el este    the east

**And:**  ésta  this

Like -este- this word is a pronoun with the accent and an adjective without the accent.

Está-is also the conjugated form of the verb -estar- to be.
e.g. usted está            you are
   el/ella está           he/she/it is

# PUNCTUATION MARKS

The Spanish language always uses inverted question and exclamation marks (¿ or ¡) as the beginning punctuation marks for all interrogative and exclamatory sentences (or clauses). These sentences will also end with the question or exclamation mark.
e.g. ¿Puede usted mover la cabeza?    Can you move your head?
   ¡No toques eso!            Do not touch that!

# REFERENCE

Numbers/ Temperature/ Months/ Seasons/ Family/ Days of the Week/ Time / Days & Dates/ Color & Clothing/ Bones of the Body.

The months of the year, the days of the week and the seasons, are not capitalized in Spanish.

## NUMBERS

## Cardinal Numbers

| 0 | cero | SEH-roh |
|---|---|---|
| 1 | uno | OOnoh |
| 2 | dos | dos |
| 3 | tres | trehs |
| 4 | cuatro | KWAH-troh |
| 5 | cinco | SEEN-koh |
| 6 | seis | sehss |
| 7 | siete | SEE-EHteh |
| 8 | ocho | OH-choh |
| 9 | nueve | NWEH-beh |
| 10 | diez | dee-es |
| 11 | once | ON-seh |
| 12 | doce | DOH-seh |
| 13 | trece | TREH-seh |
| 14 | catorce | kah-TORseh |
| 15 | quince | KEEN-seh |
| 16 | dieciséis | dee-eesee-SEHES |
| 17 | diecisiete | dee-eesee-SEE-EHteh |
| 18 | dieciocho | dee-eesee-OH-choh |
| 19 | diecinueve | dee-eesee-NWEH-beh |
| 20 | veinte | BEHNteh |
| 21 | veintiuno | behn-teeOOnoh |
| 22 | veintidos | behn-teeDOS |
| 23 | veintitrés | behn-teeTREHS |
| 24 | veinticuatro | behn-teeKWAH-troh |
| 25 | veinticinco | behn-teeSEEN-choh |
| 26 | veintiséis | behn-teeSEHSS |
| 27 | veintisiete | behn-teeSEE-EHteh |
| 28 | veintiocho | behn-teeOH-choh |
| 29 | veintinueve | behn-teeNWEH-beh |
| 30 | treinta | TREHNtah |
| 31 | treinta y uno | TREHNtah ee OOnoh |
| 32 | treinta y dos | TREHNtah ee dos |

| | | |
|---|---|---|
| 33 | treinta y tres | TREHNtah ee trehs |
| 40 | cuarenta | kwah-REHNtah |
| 41 | cuarenta y uno | kwah-REHNtah ee OOnoh |
| 50 | cincuenta | seen-KWENtah |
| 51 | cincuenta y uno | seen-KWENtah ee OOnoh |
| 60 | sesenta | seh-SEHNtah |
| 61 | sesenta y uno | seh-SEHNtah ee OOnoh |
| 70 | setenta | seh-TEHNtah |
| 71 | setenta y uno | seh-TEHNtah ee OOnoh |
| 80 | ochenta | oh-CHEHNtah |
| 81 | ochenta y uno | oh-CHEHNtah ee OOnoh |
| 90 | noventa | noh-BEHNtah |
| 91 | noventa y uno | noh-BEHNtah ee OOnoh |
| 100 | cien | SEEen |
| 101 | ciento uno | seeENtoh OOnoh |
| 110 | ciento diez | seeENtoh dee-es |
| 120 | ciento veinte | see-ENtoh BEHN-the |
| 200 | doscientos | dosSEE-ENtos |
| 300 | trescientos | trehsSEE-ENtos |
| 400 | cuatrocientos | kwahtroSEE-ENtos |
| 500 | quinientos | keeNEE-ENtos |
| 600 | seiscientos | sehssSEE-ENtos |
| 700 | setecientos | seh-tehSEE-ENtos |
| 800 | ochocientos | oh-chohSEE-ENtos |
| 900 | novecientos | noh-behSEE-ENtos |
| 1,000 | mil | meel |
| 1,100 | mil cien | meel SEE-en |
| 1,600 | mil seiscientos | meel sehssSEE-ENtos |
| 2,000 | dos mil | dos meel |
| 10,000 | diez mil | dee-es meel |
| 100,000 | cien mil | SEE-en meel |
| 1,000,000 | un millon | oon meejon |

## Ordinal Numbers

| | | |
|---|---|---|
| first | primero | preeMEH-roh |
| second | segundo | sehGOON-doh |
| third | tercero | terSEH-roh |
| fourth | cuarto | KWAR-toh |
| fifth | quinto | KEEN-toh |
| sixth | sexto | SEKS-toh |
| seventh | séptimo | SEPtee-moh |
| eighth | octavo | ohkTAH-boh |
| ninth | noveno | nobEH-noh |
| tenth | décimo | DEHsee-moh |
| eleventh | undécimo | oonDEHsee-moh |

## Fractions

| | | |
|---|---|---|
| one half | un medio OR la mitad | oon MEHdee-coh/lahMeeTAD |
| one-third | un tercio OR una tercera parte | TerSEE-oh/terSEH-rah PAR-teh |
| one-quarter | un cuarto OR. una cuarta parte | KWAR-toh/KWAR-tah PAR-teh |
| one-eighth | un octavo OR. una octava parte | ohkTAH-boh/ohkTAH-bah PAR-teh |

## Number Phrases

| | | |
|---|---|---|
| once | una vez | OOnah bes |
| twice | dos veces | dos BEHses |
| three times | tres veces | trehs BEHses |
| a half | una mitad | OOnah meeTAD |
| half of | la mital de | lah meeTAL deh... |
| one third | un tercio | oon TEHRsee-oh |
| 5.2% | cinco, dos ciento | SEENkoh (KOHmah) dos see-ENtoh |
| fifty percent | cincuenta por ciento | seen-KWENtah pohr seeENtoh |

# TEMPERATURE

| | | |
|---|---|---|
| centigrade | centígrado/a | senTEE-grah-doh/dah |
| degree | el grado | GRAH-dos |
| melting point | el punto de fusión | POON-toh deh foo-seeOHN |
| temperature | la temperatura | tem-pehr-rahTOOrah |
| tepid | tibio/a | tee-BEEoh/ah |

# MONTHS

| | | |
|---|---|---|
| January | enero | eh-NEHroh |
| February | febrero | feh-BREHroh |
| March | marzo | MAR-soh |
| April | abril | ah-BREEL |
| May | mayo | MAH-joh |
| June | junio | HOOnee-oh |
| July | julio | HOOlee-oh |
| August | agosto | ah-GOHStoh |
| September | septiembre | sep-TEE-EMbreh |
| October | octubre | ok-TOObreh |
| November | noviembre | noh-BEE-EMbreh |
| December | diciembre | dee-SEE-EMbreh |

## SEASONS

| | | |
|---|---|---|
| spring | la primavera | lah pree-mah-BEHrah |
| summer | el verano | el beh-RAHnoh |
| autumn | el otoño | el oh-TOHnyoh |
| winter | el invierno | el eenBEERnoh |

## FAMILY

| | | | |
|---|---|---|---|
| husband/wife | el esposo/a | es-pohsoh/sah | |
| son/daughter | el hijo/a | EE-hoh/hah | |
| brother/sister | el hermano/a | ehr-MAH-noh/nah | |
| father | el padre | PAHdreh | |
| mother | la madre | MAHdreh | |
| grandfather/mother | el abuelo/a | ah- BWEHloh/lah | |
| uncle/aunt | el tío | TEE-oh/ah | |
| nephew/niece | el sobrino | sohBREE-noh/nah | |
| cousin | el primo/a | PREEmoh/mah | * |
| brother/sister-in-law | el cuñado | koo-NYAHdoh/dah | |
| stepson/daughter | el hijastro/a | eeHAS-troh/trah | |
| stepbrother/sister | el hermanastro | ehr-manNAS-trah/troh | |
| stepfather | el padrastro | pahDRAS-troh | |
| stepmother | la madrastra | mahDRAS-thah | |
| ex-husband | el ex-marido | ehks- maREEdoh | |
| ex-wife | la ex-mujer | ehks-MOO-hehr | |
| grandson/daughter | el nieto | nee-EHtoh/tah | |
| boy/girlfriend | el novio | nohVEE-oh/ah | |
| fiancé/fiancée | el prometido | proh-mehTEEdoh/dah | |
| siblings | los hermanos/as | erMAH-nos/nas | # |
| son-in-law | el yerno | JEHRnoh | |
| daughter-in-law | la nuera | NWEHrah | |
| godfather | el padrino | padREEnoh | |
| godmother | la madrina | mahDREEnah | |
| great-greatgrandfather/mother | el bisabuelo | beesahBWEHloh/lah | |
| great-grandson/daughter | el bisnieto | beesNEE-eh-toh/tah | |
| guardian | el guardián/a | gar-dee-AN/ANAH | * |
| parents | los padres | pahDRES | |
| relatives | los parientes | pah-ree-EHNtes | |

\* use - a- for feminine
\# use -as- if referring to mixed male & female & -os- for all female

# PEOPLE

| | | |
|---|---|---|
| adlescent | el adolescente, la adolescente | adoh-lehs-CEHNteh |
| baby | el bebé | beh-BEH |
| boy/girl | el chico, el muchacho/a | chee-CHOH/moo-chah-CHOH/AH* |
| childeren | los niños | nee-NYOS |
| doctor | doctor/doctora | dohk-TOHR/dohk-TOHrah  # |
| friend | el amigo, la amiga | ameeGOH/GAH  * |
| gentleman/Mr. | el señor | seh-NYOR |
| lady/Mrs | la señora | seh-NYOHrah |
| man | el hombre | OHM-breh |
| old man/woman | el anciano | ahseeAHnoh/nah |
| people | la gente | GEHN-teh |
| woman | la mujer | MOO-hehr |
| young boy/girl | el niño/a | neeNYOS/NYAS  * |
| miss/young lady | señorita | seh-nyoh-REEtah |

* -o- ending for the masculine & -a- ending for the fememine
# or- ending for the masculine and -ra- ending for the feminine

# DAYS OF THE WEEK

| | | |
|---|---|---|
| Monday | lunes | LOO-nehs |
| Tuesday | martes | MAR-tehs |
| Wednesday | miércoles | MEERkoh-les |
| Thursday | jueves | HWEH-bes |
| Friday | viernes | BEE-ERnes |
| Saturday | sábado | SAHbah-doh |
| Sunday | domingo | doh-MEENgoh |

# TIME

In Spanish the hour is always said before the minutes and is always given a definite article.

| | |
|---|---|
| around | alrededor de |
| | al-reh-dehDOR deh |
| early | temprano |
| | temPRAHno |
| late | tarde |
| | tarde |
| on time | a tiempo |
| | ah teeEHMpoh |
| on the dot | en punto |
| | ehn POONtoh |

## Spanish for Radiology Professionals

| | |
|---|---|
| during the day | durante el día |
| | dooRANteh el DEE-ah |
| right now | ahora mismo |
| | ah-OHrah MEESmoh |
| morning | la mañana |
| | mah-NYAHnah |
| afternoon | la tarde |
| | TAR-deh |
| night | la noche |
| | NOH-cheh |
| second | el segundo |
| | seh-GOONdah |
| minute | el minuto |
| | mee-NOOtos |
| hour | la hora |
| | OHrah |
| day | el día |
| | DEE-ah |
| week | la semana |
| | seh-MAHnah |
| month | el mes |
| | mes |
| year | el año |
| | AH-nyoh |
| days | de día |
| | deh DEEah |
| everyday | diario OR diariamente |
| | dee-ahREEoh/dee-ah-reeah-menTEH |
| nocturnal | nocturno OR relativo a la noche |
| | nohTOORnoh/rehlahTEEvoh ah lah NOH-che |
| time | la vez, el tiempo |
| | bes/ teeEM-poh |
| What time is it? | ¿Que hora es? |
| | keh oh-rah es |
| It is ….one o'clock | Es… la una            * |
| | Es… lah oona |
| It is… | Son…            * |
| | Sohn |
| …two o'clock | …las dos |
| | las dos |
| …eight o'clock | …las ocho. |
| | las OH-choh |
| …eight fifteen. | …las ocho y cuarto. |
| | las OH-choh ee KWAR-toh |
| …eight twenty. | …las ocho y veinte. |
| | las OH-choh ee BEHNteh |
| …eight thirty. | …las ocho y media. |
| | las OH-choh ee MEH-deeah |

| | |
|---|---|
| ...eight fortyfive. | ...las nueve menos cuarto. |
| | las NWEH-beh MEH-nos KWAR-toh |
| ...nine o'clock. | ...las nueve. |
| | las NWEH-beh |
| ...nine ten. | ...las nueve y diez. |
| | las NWEH-beh ee dee-es |
| ...nine forty. | ...las diez menos veinte. |
| | las dee-es MEH-nos BEHNtheh |
| 10:15 | diez y cuarto |
| | dee-es ee KWAR-toh |
| 11:30 | once y media |
| | ON-seh ee meh-DEEah |
| nine o'clock sharp | nueve en punto |
| | NWEH-beh ehn POON-tos |
| at one o'clock | a la una |
| | ah lah oona |
| at four p.m. | a las cuatro de la tarde |
| | ah las KWAH-troh deh lah tar-deh |
| at night | por la noche |
| | pohr lah NOH-cheh |
| at noon | al mediodía |
| | al meh-dee-ohDEEah |
| at midnight | a la medianoche |
| | ah lah meh-dee-ahNOH-cheh |
| in the morning | por la mañana |
| | pohr lah mah-NYAHnah |
| in the afternoon | por la tarde |
| | pohr lah TAR-deh |
| in ten minutes | en diez minutos |
| | en dee-es mee-NOOtos |
| in 1/4 of an hour | en un cuarto de hora |
| | en oon KWAR-toh deh oh-rah |
| in 1/2 an hour | en media hora |
| | en meh-DEEah oh-rah |
| in 3/4 of an hour | en tres cuartos de hora |
| | en trehs KWAR-tos deh oh-rah |
| in the evening *(specific time)* | de la noche |
| | deh lah NOHcheh |
| in the evening *(non-specific)* | por la noche |
| | pohr lah NOHcheh |
| It's three o'clock in the afternoon. | Son las tres de la tarde. |
| | sohn las trehs deh lah TAR-deh |

\* Note that -es- is used only for the singular as with -una- and -son- is used with all the other hours.

# DAYS AND DATES

| | |
|---|---|
| date | la fecha |
| | FEH-chah |
| today | hoy |
| | oi |
| every day | todos los días |
| | TOH-dos los DEE-as |
| tonight | esta noche |
| | ES-tah NOH-cheh |
| tomorrow | mañana |
| | mah-NYAHnah |
| tomorrow evening | mañana por la tarte |
| | mah-NYAHnah pohr lah TAR-deh |
| tomorrow night | mañana por la noche |
| | mah-NYAHnah pohr lah NOH-cheh |
| tomorrow morning | mañana por la mañana |
| | mah-NYAHnah pohr lah mah-NYAHnah |
| tomorrow afternoon | mañana por la tarde |
| | mah-NYAHnah pohr lah TAR-deh |
| week | la semana |
| | lah seh-MAHnah |
| weekend | el fin de semana |
| | el feen deh seh-MAHnah |
| yesterday | ayer |
| | ah-JER |
| yesterday morning | ayer por la mañana |
| | ah-JER pohr lah mah-NYAHnah |
| yesterday afternoon | ayer por la tarde |
| | ah-JER pohr lah TAR-deh |
| after July | después de julio |
| | dehs-POOES deh HOOlee-oh |
| before Thursday/February | antes de jueves/febrero |
| | AN-tehs deh HWEH-bes/ feb-BREHroh |
| during the day | durante el día |
| | dooRANteh el DEE-ah |
| during June | durante junio |
| | dooRAN-teh HOOnee-oh |
| in March | en marzo |
| | en MAR-soh |
| on Tuesday | los martes |
| | los MAR-tes |
| this morning | esta mañana |
| | ES-tah mah-NYAHnah |
| this afternoon | esta tarde |
| | ES-tah TAR-deh |
| this year | este año |
| | ES-the AH-nyoh |

| | |
|---|---|
| this week | esta semana |
| | ES-tah seh-MAHnah |
| last night | anoche |
| | ahNOCH-cheh |
| last night | la noche pasada |
| | lah NOH-cheh pah-SAHdah |
| last week | la semana pasada |
| | lah seh-MAHnah pah-SAHdah |
| last month | el mes pasado |
| | el mes pah-SAHdah |
| last year | el año pasado |
| | el AH-nyoh pah-SAHdoh |
| last Tuesday | el martes pasado |
| | el MAR-tehs pah-SAHdah |
| last Wednesday | el miércoles |
| | el MEERkoh-les |
| two days ago | hace dos días |
| | AH-seh dos DEE-as |
| the day before | el día anterior |
| | el DEE-ah an-tehREE-OR |
| the day before yesterday | anteayer |
| | an-teh-ahJER |
| the day after tomorrow | pasado mañana |
| | pah-SAHdoh mah-NYAHnah |
| the night before last | anteanoche |
| | an-teh-ah-NOH-cheh |
| the next day | el día siguiente |
| | el DEE-ah seeGIH-ENteh |
| next month | el próximo mes OR el mes que viene |
| | PROKsee-moh mes/ mes keh veeEN-eh |
| next week | la próxima semana OR la semana que viene |
| | PROKsee-mah seh-MAHnah/seh-MAHnah veeEN-eh |
| the next year | el próximo año /el año que viene |
| | PROKsee-moh AH-nyoh/ AH-nyoh keh veeEN-eh |
| next Monday | el próximo lunes OR el lunes que viene |
| | PROKsee-moh LOO-nehs/ LOO-nehs keh veeEN-eh |
| next Tuesday | el martes que viene OR el próximo martes |
| | el MAR-tehs keh veeEN-eh/ el PROKseemoh MAR-tehs |
| Monday through Friday | de lunes a viernes |
| | deh LOO-nes ah veeEHRnes |
| It is the 1st of January. | Hoy es el primero de enero          * |
| | oi es el pree-MEHroh de eh-NEHroh |
| Today is Monday | Hoy es lunes. |
| | oi es LOO-nes |
| What is today's date? | ¿Qué fecha es hoy? |
| | keh FEH-chah es oi |

## Spanish for Radiology Professionals

| | |
|---|---|
| in two minutes | en dos minutos |
| | en dos mee-NOOtos |
| in four hours | en cuatro horas |
| | en KWAH-troh OHR-ahs |
| in 3 days time | en tres días |
| | en trehs DEE-as |
| in 2 days time | en dos días |
| | en dos DEE-as |
| in the morning (*specific time*) | de la mañana |
| | deh lah mah-NYAHnah |
| in the morning (*non-specific*) | por la mañana |
| | pohr lah mah-NYAHnah |
| in the afternoon (*specific time*) | de la tarde |
| | deh lah TAR-deh |
| in the afternoon (*non- specific*) | por la tarde |
| | pohr lah TAR-deh |
| since April | desde abril |
| | DEHS-deh ah-BREEL |
| not until May | no hasta mayo |
| | noh AS-tah MAH-joh |
| the beginning of August | principios de agosto |
| | preen-SEEpeeos deh ah-GOHStoh |
| the middle of September | mediados de septiembre |
| | meh-DEEah-dos deh sep-TEE-EMbreh |
| the end of October | finales de octubre |
| | feen-AHles deh ok-TOObreh |
| in 1990 | en mil novecientos noventa |
| | en meel noh-behSEE-ENtos noh-BEHNtah |
| 1992 | mil novecientos noventa y dos |
| | meel noh-behSEE-ENtos noh-BEHNtah ee dos |
| in 2010 | en dos mil y diez |
| | en dos meel ee dee-es |
| in 2011 | en dos mil y once |
| | en dos meel ee On-seh |

\* The ordinal number -primero- is used when referring to the first day of the month.

# COLOR AND CLOTHING

## Color

| | | |
|---|---|---|
| black | negro | NEH-groh |
| blue | azul | ah-SOOL |
| brown | marrón, café | mah-RON, cah-FEH |
| green | verde | BER-deh |
| grey | gris | grees |
| orange | naranja, anaranjado | nah-RANhah, ah-nahran-HAHdoh |
| pink | rosado | roh-SAHdoh |
| purple | purpúra | poor-POOrah |
| red | rojo | ROH-hoh |
| silver | de plata, plateado | deh PLAH-tah, plah-tehAHdoh |
| white | blanco | BLAN-koh |
| yellow | amarillo | ah-mahREEjoh |
| light | claro | KLAH-roh |
| dark | oscuro | os-KOOroh |
| corduroy | pana | PAH-nah |
| cotton | algodón | al-gohDON |
| leather | cuero | KWEH-roh |
| silk | seda | SEH-deh |
| wool | lana | LAH-nah |
| artificial | artificial | ar-tee-feeSEE-AL |
| synthetic | sintético | seen-TEHtee-coh |

## Clothing

| | | |
|---|---|---|
| bag | la cartera | kahr-TEHrah |
| belt | la correa, la cinto | kohREH-ah, SEEN-toh |
| blouse | la blusa, la camisa | BLOO-sah, kahMEE-sah |
| boot | la bota | BOH-tah |
| bra | el sostén | sohs-TEN |
| bracelet | la pulsera | poolSEH-rah |
| cap | el/lagorro/a | GOH-roh/ah |
| chains | las cadenas | kahDEH-nas |
| clothes | la ropa | ROH-pah |
| clothing | el camisón | kah-meeSON |

| | | |
|---|---|---|
| coat | la capa | KAH-pah |
| dress | el vestido | besTEE-doh |
| dressing gown | la bata | BAH-tah |
| earrings | los pantallas | panTAH-jas |
| glove | el guante | GWAN-the |
| hairpin/clip | la pinche de pelo | PEEN-cheh deh PEH-loh |
| hat | el sombrero | somBREH-roh, |
| | el gorro | GOH-roh |
| jacket | el chaqueta | chah-KEHtah |
| jeans | los vaqueros | bah-KEHros |
| jewelry | la joyería | hoh-jehREE-ah |
| | la prenda | PREN-dah |
| necklace | el collar | koh-JAHR |
| nightdress | el camisón | kah-meeSON |
| panties | las bragas | BRAH-gas |
| pants | los pantalones | pan-tah-LOHnes |
| panty-hose | la media pantalón | meh-DEEah pan-tahLON |
| raincoat | la capa | KAH-pah |
| | el impermeable | eem-per-mehAH-bleh |
| ring | la sortija | sorTEE-hah |
| sandal | la chancleta | chan-KLEHtah |
| | la zapatilla | sah-pahTEE-jah |
| shirt | la camiseta | kah-meeSEH-tah |
| | la camisa | kah-MEEsah |
| shoe | el zapato | sah-PAHtoh |
| shorts | los calzoncillos | kal-sohnSEEjos |
| skirt | la falda | FAHL-dah |
| sock/stocking | la media | meh-DEEah |
| slipper | la chancleta | chan-KLEHtah |
| sneaker | la tenis | TEH-nees |
| stocking | la pantaleta | pan-tahLEH-tah |
| sweater | el suéer | SWEH-ter |
| tie | la corbata | kor-BAHtah |
| undershirt | la camiseta | kah-meeSEHtah |
| underwear | la ropa interior | ROH-pah een-TEHReeor |
| wrist-watch | el reloj de pulsera | reh-LOH deh pool-SEHRrah |
| zipper | el zipper | see-PEHR |
| | la cremallera | kreh-mah-JERrah |

# BONES & BODY PARTS

| | | |
|---|---|---|
| abdomen | el abdomen | ab-DOHmen |
| ankle | el tobillo | toh-BEEjoh |
| anus | el ano | AH-noh |
| arm | el brazo | BRAH-soh |
| artery | la arteria | ar-tehREE-ah |
| back | la espalda | es-PALdah |
| breast | el seno | SEH-noh |
| bladder | la vejiga | beh-HEEgah |
| blood vessels | el vasos sanguíneos | BAH-sos san-GIHneh-os |
| bone | el hueso | oo-EHsoh |
| body | el cuerpo | KWER-poh |
| bowels | los intestinos | een-tesTEEnos |
| cervical spine | la espina cervicales | es-PEEnah ser-bee-KAHles |
| cheek | la mejilla | meh-HEEjah |
| chest | el pecho | PEH-choh |
| chin | la quijada | kee-HAHdah |
| clavicle | la clavícula | klah-BEEkoo-lah |
| coccyx | el coccis | KOK-sees |
| coccyx bone | el hueso coxal | oo-EHsoh koks-AL |
| colon | el colon | KOH-lon |
| diaphragm | el diafragma | deeah-FRAGmah |
| ear | el oído | oh-EEdoh |
| elbow | el codo | KOH-doh |
| esophagus | el esófago | eh-SOHfah-goh |
| eye | el ojo | OH-hoh |
| face | la cara | KAH-rah |
| femur | el femur | feh-MOOR |
| fibula | la fíbula | FEEboo-lah |
| fingers | el/los dedo/s de la mana | DEH-doh/os deh lahMAH-nah |
| foot | el pie | PEE-eh |
| forearm | el antebrazo | an-teh-BRAHsoh |
| forehead | la frente | FREN-teh |
| gall bladder | vesicula biliar | behSEE-koo-lah bee-leeAR |
| gland | la glandula | glan-DOOlah |
| groin | ingúinal area | een-GIHnal ah-REEah |
| hair | el pelo | PEH-loh |
| hand | la mano | MAH-noh |
| head | la cabeza | kah-BEEsah |
| heart | el corazón | koh-rahSON |
| heel | el talón | tah-LON |
| hip | la cadera | kah-DEHrah |
| intestine | el intestino | een-tes-TEEnoh |
| jaws | la mandibula | man-dee-BOOlah |
| joint | la articulación | ar-tee-koo-lahSEEON |
| kidney | el/los riñón/es | ree-NYON/es |

## Spanish for Radiology Professionals

| English | Spanish | Pronunciation |
|---|---|---|
| knee | la rodilla | ro-DEEjah |
| large bowels | el intestino grueso | een-tes-TEEnoh GRWEH-soh |
| leg | la pierna | PEE-ERnah |
| lip | la labio | lah-BEEoh |
| liver | el hígado | EEgah-doh |
| lower arm | parte de abajo del brazo | PAR-teh...ah-BAH-hoh del BRAH-soh |
| lumbar spine | la espina lumbar | loom-BAR |
| lungs | el/los pulmon/es | pool-MOHN/es |
| mandible | la mandíbula | man-DEEboo-lah |
| mastoids | la mastoide | mas-TOYdeh |
| mastoid bone | el hueso mastoideo | oo-EHsoh mas-TOYdee-oh |
| maxilla | el/los maxila/res | maks-EElah/res |
| maxilla bone | el hueso maxilar | maks-EElar |
| mouth | la boca | BOH-kah |
| muscle | el músculo | MOOSkoo-loh |
| nasal bone | el hueso nasal | nah-SAL |
| neck | el cuello | KWEH-joh |
| nerve | el nervio | ner-BEEoh |
| nervous system | el sistema nervioso | seesTEHmah ner-beeOH-soh |
| nose | la naríz | nah-REES |
| orbits | las orbitas | ORbee-tah |
| paranasal sinuses | los senos/paranasales | SEH-nos pah-rah-nah-SAHles |
| · ethmoid | etmoidales | et-moy-DAHles |
| · sphenoid | esfenoidales | es-feh-noy-DAHles |
| · frontal | frontales | fron-TAHles |
| · maxillary | maxilares | mahks-ee-LARes |
| pelvis | la pelvis | PEL-bees |
| pelvis bones | los huesos pelvico | oo-EHsoh PELbees-koh |
| penis | el pene | PEH-neh |
| ribs | las costillas | kos-TEEjas |
| shoulder | el hombro | OHM-broh |
| sinuses | los senos | SEH-nos |
| skin | la piel | pee-EL |
| skull | el cráneo | CRAHneh-oh |
| small bowels | el intestino delgado | een-tes-TEEnoh del-GAHdoh |
| spine | la espina | es-PEEnah |
| stomach | estómago | es-TOHmah-goh |
| sole (of feet) | la planta (del pie) | PLAN-tah ... PEE-eh |
| sacrum | el sacro | SAK-roh |
| sacrum bone | el hueso sacral | SAK-cral |
| tendon | el tendon | TEN-dohn |
| thigh | el muslo | MOOS-loh |
| thoracic spine | la espina torácica | es-PEEnah toh-RAHsee-kah |
| throat | la garganta | gar-GANtah |
| thumb | el dedo pulgar | DEH-doh pool-GAR |
| tibia | la tibia | tee-BEEah |
| toe | el dedo del pie | DEH-doh ...PEE-eh |
| tongue | la lengua | LEHN-gwah |

*35*

| | | |
|---|---|---|
| tonsils | las tonsilos | ton-SEElos |
| upper arm | parte de arriba del brazo | PAR-teh deh ah-REEbah del BRAH-soh |
| upper leg | parte superior de la pierna | PAR-teh soo-peh-REEor deh lah PEE-ERnah |
| ureter | el uréter | oo-REHter |
| vein | la vena | BEH-nah |
| vagina | la vagina | bah-GEEnah |
| waist | la cintura | seen-TOOrah |
| wrist | la muñeca | moo-NYEHkah |

# GENERAL GREETINGS

| | |
|---|---|
| Hello. | Hola.<br>OH-lah |
| Good morning. | Buenos dias<br>BWEN-os DEE-as |
| Good afternoon. | Buenas tardes<br>BWEN-as TAR-des |
| Good night. | Buenas noches.<br>BWEN-as NOH-chehs |
| Goodbye /See you later. | Adiós /Hasta luego.<br>ah-deeOOS / AS-tah LWEH-goh |
| Excuse me. | Perdóneme/Excúseme.<br>per-DOHneh-meh/eks-KOOseh-meh |
| How are you? | ¿Cómo está usted?<br>KOH-moh es-TAH oosTED |
| Nice to meet you. | Mucho gusto.<br>MOOCH-oh GOOS-toh |
| I'm sorry. | Lo siento<br>loh seeEN-toh |
| Please. | Por favor<br>pohr fah-BOHR |
| Thank you. | Gracias<br>GRAHsee-as |
| Thank you very much. | Muchas gracias<br>MOO-chas GRAHsee-as |
| Yes/No | Sí/No<br>see/noh |
| Yes/No... Thank you | Sí/No... Gracias<br>see/noh...GRAHsee-as |
| Yes/No... Please | Sí/No... Por favor<br>see/noh...pohr fah-BOHR |

| | |
|---|---|
| A pleasure. | Un placer<br>oon plah-SEHR |
| You're welcome. | De nada /Está bien.<br>deh NAH-dah /es-TAH beeEN |
| The pleasure is mine. | El placer es mio.<br>el plah-SEHR es MEE-oh |
| Very well /Fine thanks, | uy bien/ Muy bien gracias,<br>mooee beeEN /mooee been GRAHsee-as, |
| ...and you? | ...¿y usted?<br>...ee oosTED |

# USEFUL QUESTIONS AND EXPRESSIONS

| | |
|---|---|
| Anything else? | ¿Algo más? <br> AL-goh mas |
| Is that all? | ¿Eso es todo...? <br> ES-oh es TOH-doh |
| This one | Éste (m), ésta (f), esto (n) # <br> ES-teh, ES-tah, ES-toh |
| That one | Ése <br> ES-eh |
| Those (for something near) | Ésos (m), ésas (f) # <br> ES-ohs, ES-ahs |
| Those (distant) | Aquéllos (m), aquéllas (f) # <br> Ah-KEHjohs, ah-KEHjahs |
| How? | ¿Cómo? <br> KOH-moh |
| How much? | ¿Cuánto/a? <br> QWAN-toh/tah |
| How many? | ¿Cuántos/as? <br> QWAN-tos/tas |
| How many times? | ¿Cuántas veces? <br> QWAN-tas BEH-sehs |
| How often? | ¿Cada cuándo? <br> KAH-dah QWAN-doh |
| How old are you | ¿Cuántos años tienes? <br> QWAN-tas AH-nyoh teeEHNes |
| What? | ¿Qué? <br> KEH |
| What happened? | ¿Qué pasó/occurrio? <br> KEH pahSOH/ohKOORreh-oh |
| What hurts? | ¿Qué le duele? <br> KEH leh DWEH-leh |

| | |
|---|---|
| What did you take/drink/eat? | ¿Qué tomó usted/bebió ud/comié ud?<br>KEH tohMOH oosTED/beh-beeOH/coh-meeEH |
| Of what? | ¿De qué?<br>deh KEH |
| When? | ¿Cuándo?<br>QWAN-doh |
| Where? | ¿Dónde?<br>DON-deh |
| Where to? | ¿Adónde?<br>ah-DONdeh |
| Where from? | ¿De dónde?<br>Deh DONdeh |
| Where are you/they? | ¿Dónde está?/estan<br>DON-deh esTAH/EStahn |
| Where do you live? | ¿Dóndevive?<br>DONdeh BEHveh |
| Why? | ¿Por qué?<br>pohr KEH |
| Who? | ¿Quién? (pl. ¿Quienes?)<br>kee-EN /kee-enNES |
| Whose? | ¿De quién?<br>deh kee-EN |
| To whom? | ¿A quién? (pl. ¿A quienes?)<br>ah kee-EN/ ah kee-enNES |
| With whom? | ¿Con quién? (pl. ¿Con quienes?)<br>con keeEN/con kee-enNES |
| Which? | ¿Cuál?/¿Cuáles?<br>kwal/KWAH-les |
| Which ones? | ¿Cuales?<br>KWAH-les |
| Is there? Are there? | ¿Hay?<br>ahee |

## Spanish for Radiology Professionals

| | |
|---|---|
| Is there?/Are there? | ¿Hay?<br>ahee |
| Where are...?/What is...? | ¿Dónde están...?/¿Qué es...?<br>DON-deh es-TAN...?/KEH es...? |
| Come in. | Entra.<br>EN-trah |
| I know. | Sé.<br>SEH |
| I don't know. | No sé.<br>noh SEH |
| I understand. | Comprendo /Entiendo.<br>kom-PRENdoh /en-teeEN-doh |
| I don't understand. | No comprendo.<br>noh kom-PRENdoh |
| I do not speak Spanish. | No hablo español.<br>noh AB-loh es-pah-NYOL |
| I do not understand Spanish. | No comprendo español.<br>noh kom-PRENdoh es-pah-NYOL |
| I speak only a little Spanish. | Sólo hablo un poco de español.<br>SOH-loh AB-loh oon POH-koh deh es-pah-NYOH |
| I will get someone to translate for you. | Puedo buscar algún interprete para usted.<br>PWEH-doh boos-CAR al-GOON eenter-PREHteh PAH-rah oosTED |
| I will try to help you. | Voy a tratar de ayudarle<br>voy ah trah-TAR deh ah-joo-ARleh |
| I will be back soon. | Regreso pronto.<br>reh-GREHsoh pron toh |
| Do you understand? | ¿Comprende usted?<br>kom-PRENdeh oosTED |
| Do you understand? | ¿Entiende Usted?<br>en-teeEN-deh oosTED |
| Do you prefer ...? | ¿Prefiere usted ...?<br>Preh-feeEHreh oosTED |

| | |
|---|---|
| How can I help you? | ¿En qué puedo ayudarle?<br>en KEH PWEH-doh ah-joo-DARleh |
| Please sit down... | Por favor, siéntese...<br>pohr fah-BOHR, seeEN-teh-seh |
| ...here *(point)*. | ...aquí.<br>ah-KEE |
| ...over here. | ...acá.<br>ah-KAH |
| ...there *(point)* | ...allí.<br>ah-JEE |
| ...over there *(point)* | ...allá.<br>ah-JAH |
| Please wait here. | Por favor, espere aquí.<br>pohr fah-BOOR, es-PEERreh ah-KEE |
| Have you paid for this? | ¿Tuvo que pagar por esto?<br>TOO-boh keh pah-GAR pohr ES-toh |
| This test is free. | Este estudio es gratis.<br>ES-teh es-TOOdee-oh es GRAH-tees |
| Here is the receipt. | Aquí está el recibo.<br>ah-KEE es-TAH el reh-SEEboh |
| Someone will be with you shortly. | Alguien estará con usted pronto<br>AHL-giehn es-tahRAH con oosTED PRON-toh |
| The cashier is over there. | La caja está allí.<br>lah KAH-ah es-TAH ah-JEE |
| One moment please... | Un momento, por favor...<br>oon moh-MENtoh, pohr fah-BOHR |
| Will that be all...? | ¿Será eso todo...?<br>seh-RAH ES-oh TOH-doh |
| You are in the department. | Usted está en el departamento<br>oosTED es-TAH en el deh-partah-MENtoh |
| Could you please...? | ¿Por favor podría usted...?<br>pohr fah-BOHR poh-DREEah oosTED.. |

## Spanish for Radiology Professionals

| | |
|---|---|
| ...repeat that? | ...repetir eso?<br>reh-pehTEER ES-oh |
| ...repeat that in English? | ...repita eso en inglés?<br>reh-PIHtah ES-oh en een-GLEHS |
| ...speak more slowly? | ...hablar más despacio?<br>ab-LAR mas des-PAHseeoh |
| ...write that down | ...escribalo aquí?<br>eskree-BAHloh ah-KEE |
| No smoking please. | No fume, por favor.<br>noh FOO-meh pohr fah-BOHR |
| Please put out the... | Apague...por favor<br>ah-PAHkeh...pohr fah-BOHR |
| ...cigarette | ...el cigarrillo<br>el seegah-REEjoh |
| ...the cigar | ...el cigarro<br>el see-GAHroh |
| ...the pipe | ...la pipa<br>lah PEE-pah |
| Have you got...? | ¿Cogió usted...?<br>koh-geeOH oosTED |
| ...your request? | ...su requisición?<br>soo reh-kee-zee-SEEON |
| ...your receipt? | ...su recibo?<br>soo reh-SEEboh |
| ...any medical insurance? | ...seguro médico?<br>see-GOOroh MEHdee-coh |
| ...identification? | ...identificación?<br>eeden-teefee-kah-SEEON |
| Can I have...please? | ¿Puedo tener...por favor?<br>PWEH-doh teh-NEHR...pohr fah-BOHR |
| ...the x-ray request? | ...la requisición de radiografía?<br>lah reh-kee-zee-SEEON deh rah-deeoh-grah-FEEah |

| | |
|---|---|
| May I see... your request? | ¿Me deja ver... su requisición?<br>me DEH-hah ber... soo reh-kee-zee-SEEON |
| May I see...? | ¿Puedo ver...?<br>PWEH-doh ber |
| You are in the wrong department. | Usted está el departamento equivocado<br>oosTED es-TAH el deh-partah-ENtoh ehkee-boh-KAHdoh |
| Do you know what study you are having today? | ¿Sabe usted qué estudio tiene hoy?<br>SAH-beh oosTED KEH es-TOOdee-oh teeEN-eh oi |
| Did you drive here? | ¿Guió usted para venir acá?<br>gih-OH oosTED PAR-ah ben-EER ah-KAH |
| Did you come alone? | ¿Vino usted sólo(a)? *<br>BEE-noh oosTED SOH-loh(ah) |
| Did anyone accompany you here? | ¿Alguien lo/a acompañó para venir aca? *<br>AHL-giehn loh/lah ah-kom-pahNYOH PAH-rah BEN-eer ah-KAH |
| Can I make you another appointment? | ¿Puedo fijar otra cita?<br>PWEH-doh fee-HAR OHT-rah SEE-tah |
| Your next appointment is on Wednesday. | Su próxima cita es el miércoles.<br>Soh PROKsee-moh SEE-tah el MEERkoh-les |
| I am sorry, you are late. | Lo siento, pero llegó tarde<br>loh seeEN-toh PEH-rohjeh-GOH TAR-deh |
| Your appointment has been cancelled. | Su cita ha sido cancelada.<br>soo SEE-tah ah SEE-doho kan-seh-LAHdah |
| On what date is your appointment? | ¿Qué fecha tiene su cita?<br>KEH FEH-chah teeEN-eh soo SEE-tah |
| These test are by appointment only. | Estos estudios son con cita solamente.<br>ES-tos ehs-tooDEEohs son kon SEE-tah soh-lah-MENteh |

## *Spanish for Radiology Professionals* 45

| | |
|---|---|
| We tried to contact you by phone to cancel your appointment. | Nosotros tratamos de comunicarnos con usted por el teléfono para cancelar su cita.<br>noh-SOtros treh-TAHmos deh kohmoonee-CARnos con oosTED pohr el tehLEH-foh-noh PAH-rah kan-sehLAR soo SEE-tah |
| We were unable to contact you to cancel your appointment. | No pudimos comunicarnos con usted para cancelar su cita.<br>no poo-DEEmos koh-moonee-CARnos con oosTED PAH-rah kan-sehLAR soo SEE-tah |
| What time is your appointment? | ¿A qué hora es su cita?<br>ah KEH OH-rah es soo SEE-tah |
| Please take ...this | Por favor coge ...esto<br>pohr fah-BOHR KOH-geh ...ES-toh |
| ...this card. | ...esta tarjeta.<br>ES-tah tar-HEHEtah |
| ...this report. | ...esto reporte.<br>Es-toh reh-POHR-teh |
| Please take this... | Por favor lleve esto...<br>pohr fah-BOHR JEH-beh ES-toh |
| ...to the Nuclear Medicine dept. | ...al departamento de medicina nuclear.<br>al deh-partah MENtoh dc mch-dcc-SEEnah noo-clehAR |
| ...to the Ultrasound dept. | ...al departamento de ultrasonido.<br>al deh-partah-MENtoh deh ool-trah-soh-NEEdoh |
| ...to the M.R.I. Dept. | ...al departamento de resonancia magnética.<br>al deh-partah-MENtoh dehrehsoh-NAN-seeah magNEH-teekah |
| ...to the lab | ...al laboratorio<br>al laboh-rah-TOHree-oh |
| ...to the emergency room. | ...a sala de emergencia<br>ah SAH-lah deheh-mer-HENsee-ah |

| | |
|---|---|
| ...to your doctor. | ...a su doctor<br>ah soo dohk-TOHR |
| ...to the cashier. | ...a la caja<br>ah lah KAH-ah |
| This is... | Esto es...<br>ES-toh es... |
| ...your x-ray request. | ...su orden de rayos X.<br>soo OR-den deh RAH-jos EH-kees |
| ...your medical insurance card. | ...su tarjeta de seguro medico.<br>soo tar-HEHtah deh seh-GOOroh MEHdee-coh |
| ...your result. | ...su resultado.<br>soo reh-sool-TAHdoh |
| ...your x-ray. | ...su radiografía/ su placa.<br>soo rah-deeoh-grah-FEEah / soo PLA-kah |
| The tests are positive/negative. | Las pruebas son positivas/ negativas.<br>Las prooWEH-bas son poh-see-TEEvas/neh-gahTEEvas |
| The doctor will give you the results of your test. | El doctor le dará los resultados de su estudio<br>el dohk-TOHR leh DAR-rah los reh-sool-TAHdos deh soo es-TOOdee-oh |
| ...in a few days. | ...en unos dias<br>en OOnos DEE-as |
| ...in three days time. | ...en tres días.<br>en trehs DEE-as |
| ...next week. | ...la semana próxima.<br>lah seh-MAHnah PROKsee-mah |
| ...tomorrow. | ...mañana.<br>mah-NYAHnah |
| Call your doctor ... | Llame a su doctor ...<br>jah-meh ah soo dohk-TOHR... |
| ...in two days. | ...en dos días.<br>en dos DEE-as |

| | |
|---|---|
| ...if you feel worse. | ...si se siente peor.<br>see seh seeEN-teh peh-OHR |
| ...if you feel no better. | ...si no se siente mejor.<br>see noh seh seeEN-teh meh-HOHR |
| ...in the morning. | ...por la mañana.<br>pohr la mah-NYAHnah |
| You cannot exit from here. | Usted no puede salir de aquí.<br>oosTED noh PWEH-deh sah-LEER deh ah-KEE |
| Please close the door. | Por favor, cierre la puerta.<br>pohr fah-BOHR, see-EHReh lah PWER-tah |
| Do not eat or drink anything on... | No coma ni beba nada en...<br>no KOH-mah nee BEHbah NAH-dah en |
| ... the day before your study. | ...el día antes de su estudío.<br>el DEE-ah AN-tehs deh soo es-tooDEE-oh |
| ... the evening before your study. | ...la noche antes de su estudío.<br>lah NOH-cheh AN-tehs deh soo es-tooDEE-oh |
| ...the day of your study. | ...el día de su estudio<br>el DEE-ah deh soo es-TOOdee-oh |

\# -m- masculine, -f- feminine, -n- neutral

∞ está? Singular /estan pleural

\* Use -o- for masculine and -a- for feminine

@ The correct Spanish word is -radiografia- but -placa- is commonly used.

# UNDERSTANDING YOUR PATIENT

## GENERAL QUESTIONS AND EXPRESSIONS

Do you speak Spanish?
¿Habla usted español?
AB-lah oosTED es-pah-NYOL

Does anyone here speak Spanish?
¿Alguien aquí habla español?
AHL-giehn ah-KEE AB-lah es-pah-NYOL

At what time do you close/open?
¿A qué hora cierran/abren?
ah KEH OH-rah see-EHran/ah-BREN

At what time does...open.
¿A qué hora abren...?
ah KEH OH-rah ah-BREN...

...the x-ray dept.
...el departmento de rayos x
el deh-partah-MENtoh deh RAH-jos EH-kees

At what time does the doctor arrive?
¿A qué hora llega el doctor?
ah KEH OH-rah JEH-gah el dohk-TOHR

I do not understand English.
No comprendo inglés.
noh komPREN-doh een-GLEHS

I need...
Necesito...
neh-seh-SEEtoh

I would like...
Quiero...
kee-EERoh

Is...(name)... here?
¿Es...aquí?
Es...ah-KEE

I am looking for...
Estoy buscando...
es-toy boos-KANdoh

I need an appointment.
Nesito una cita.
nehSEEtoh oona SEEtah

I have an appointment with...
Tengo una cita con...
TEHN-goh OOna SEE-tah kon...

# Spanish for Radiology Professionals

| | |
|---|---|
| Can I have an appointment...? | ¿Me puede dar una cita...?<br>meh PWEH-deh dar oona SEE-tah |
| ...right now? | ...inmediatamente?<br>een-mehdee-atah-MENteh |
| ...as soon as possible? | ...tan pronto como sea posible?<br>tan PRON-toh KOH-moh SEH-ah pos-EEBleh |
| ...tomorrow? | ...mañana?<br>mah-NYAHnah |
| Can my daughter/son stay with me? | ¿Puede mi hija/o * quedarse conmigo?<br>PWEH-deh mee EE-hah/oh keh-DARseh kohn-MEEgoh |
| Can my daughter come in? | ¿Puede mi hija entrar?<br>PWEH-doh mee EE-ha en-TRAHR |
| Can you help me? | ¿Me pueden ayudar?<br>meh PWEH-den ah-joo-DAR |
| Can I use this telephone? | ¿Puedo utilizar este teléfono?<br>PWEH-doh oo-tee-leeSAR ES-teh tehLEH-foh-noh |
| Can I return... | ¿Puedo regresar...<br>PWEH-doh reh-grehSAR... |
| ...on Monday? | ...el lunes?<br>el LOO-nes |
| ...tomorrow? | ...mañana?<br>mah-NYAH-nah |
| I am here. | Estoy aquí.<br>es-toy ah-KEE |
| I am in the office. | Estoy en la oficina<br>es-toy en lah oh-feeSEEnah |
| I can't come... | No puedo venir...<br>noh PWEH-doh ben-EER |
| ...this week. | ...esta semana.<br>esTAH seh-MAHnah |
| I can come ... | Puedo venir...<br>PWEH-doh ben-EER |

| | |
|---|---|
| ..on Tuesday. | ...el martes.<br>el MAR-tehs |
| ...when you want. | ...cuando usted quiera.<br>QWAN-doh oosTED kee-EERah |
| I want to leave at ... | Yo quiero salir a...<br>joh kee-EERoh sal-EER ah... |
| ...2 o'clock. | ...las dos.<br>las dohs |
| Is this the emergency room? | ¿Es éste la sala de emergencia?<br>es ES-teh lah SAH-lah deh eh-mer-HENsee-ah |
| Is there...near by? | ¿Hay...cerca?<br>ahee...SER-kah |
| ...a bathroom... | ...un baño...<br>oon BAH-nyoh... |
| ...a coffee shop... | ...una tienda de café...<br>OOna teeEN-dah deh kah-FEH... |
| ...a cafeteria... | ...una cafetería...<br>OOna cah-feh-teh-REEah... |
| ...an information desk... | ...una mesa de información...<br>OOna MEH-sah deh een-for-mah-SEEON |
| Is it far from here? | ¿Está muy lejos de aquí?<br>es-TAH mooee LEH-hos deh ah-KEE |
| May I come in? | ¿Puedo entrar?<br>PWEH-doh en-TRAHR |
| May I speak to ...? | ¿Puedo hablar con...?<br>PWEH-doh AB-lar con |
| May one ... | ¿Se puede ...<br>seh PWEH-deh |
| ...smoke here? | ...fumar un cigarrillo aquí?<br>foo-MAR oon seegah-REEjoh ah-KEE |

## *Spanish for Radiology Professionals*

| | |
|---|---|
| ...wait here? | ...espere aquí?<br>es-peh-REH ah-KEE |
| ...get something to eat here? | ...buscar algo para comer aquí?<br>boos-CAR AL-goh PAH-rah kom-EHR ah-KEE |
| ...get out this way? | ...salir por aquí?<br>sal-EER pohr ah-KEE |
| Please may I have... | Por favor puedo tener...<br>pohr fah-BOHR PWEH-doh teh-NEHR... |
| Please, where can I get... | Por favor, dónde puedo obtener...<br>pohr fah-BOHR, DON-deh PWEH-doh ob-tehNEHR |
| Please may I have...? | ¿Por favor puedo tener...?<br>pohr fah-BOHR PWEH-doh ten-NEHR... |
| Please where can I get... | Por favor, ¿dónde puedo obtener...<br>pohr fah-BOHR, DON-dehPWEH-doh ob-tenNEHR |
| ...my blood pressure taken? | ...mi presión sanguínea?<br>mee preh-SEEon san-GIHneh-ah |
| On what floor is the doctor | En que piso esta el doctor/doctora   *<br>ehn keh PEEsoh EStah el doc-TOHR/doc-TOHrah |
| Where is...? | ¿Dónde está...?<br>DON-deh es-TAH |
| ...the bathroom? | ... el baño?<br>el BAH-nyoh |
| ...the changing/dressing room? | ...el cuarto de cambiarse<br>el QWAR-toh deh kam-BEEAR-seh |
| Where can I make a telephone call? | ¿Dónde puedo llamar por teléfono?<br>DON-deh PWEH-doh jah-MAR pohr tehLEH-foh-noh |
| Where can I find...? | ¿Dónde puedo encontrar   ...?<br>DON-deh PWEH-doh ehn-kohnTRAHR |

| | |
|---|---|
| ... the public telephone ? | ...el teléfono público?<br>el tehLEH-foh-noh POOBleek-oh |
| Where is...? | ¿Dónde está...?<br>DON-deh es-TAH |
| Where can I find/get...? | ¿Dónde puedo encontrar/conseguir...?<br>DON-deh PWEH-doh en-kohnTRAHR/<br>kohn-sehGEER |
| Can you direct me to...? | ¿Puedo usted indicarme la dirección a...?<br>PWEH-doh oosTED een-dee-CARmeh<br>lah dee-rek-SEEON ah... |
| How do I get there? | ¿Cómo puedo llegar allí?<br>KOH-moh PWEH-doh JEH-gar ah-JEE |
| How much is it? | ¿Cuánto es?<br>QWAN-toh es |
| How do I get to...? | ¿Para ir...<br>PAH-rah eer |
| ...una cafeteria? | OOna cah-feh-teh-REEah? |
| How do I get out? | ¿Cómo puedo salir?<br>KOH-moh PWEH-doh sal-EER |
| How do I get... | ¿Cómo puedo llegar...<br>KOH-moh PWEH-doh jeh-GAHR |
| ...to the x-ray dept? | ...al departamento de rayos x?<br>al deh-partah-MENtoh deh RAH-jos<br>EH-kees |
| ...to the pharmacy? | ...a la farmácia?<br>ah lah far-MAHseeah |
| ...to the lab? | ...al laboratorio?<br>al lah-boh-rah-TOHree-oh |
| ...to the first floor? | ...al primer piso?<br>al pree-MEHR PEE-soh |
| ...to the stairs? | ...a las escaleras?<br>a las es-kah-LEHras |
| ...to the emergency room? | ...a la sala de emergencia?<br>a lah SAH-lah deh eh-mer-HENsee-ah |

## *Spanish for Radiology Professionals*

| | |
|---|---|
| ...to the coffee shop? | ...a la tiendita de café?<br>a lah tee-en-DEEtah deh kah-FEH |
| ...to the billing dept? | al departamento de cobro?<br>al deh-partah-MENtoh deh KOHB-roh |
| ...to the Nuclear Medicine dept? | ...al departamento de medicina nuclear?<br>al deh-partah-MENtoh de meh-dee-SEEnah noo-clehAR |
| ...to the Ultrasound dept? | ...al departamento de ultrasonido?<br>al deh-partah-MENtoh deh ool-trah-soh-NEEdoh |
| ...to the M.R.I. Dept? | ...al departamento de resonancia magnética?<br>al deh-partah-MENtoh deh rehsoh-NAN-seeah magNEH-teekah |
| Where do I pay? | ¿Dónde pago?<br>DON-deh PAH-goh |
| Do I pay here? | ¿Tengo que pagar aquí?<br>TEHN-goh KEH PAH-gar ah-KEE |
| Do you take ... | ¿Coje usted...<br>koh-HEH oosTED |
| ...credit cards? | ...tarjeta de credito?<br>tar-HEHtah deh kreh-DEEtoh |
| ...money only? | ...dinero solamente?<br>dee-NEHroh soh-lah-MENteh |
| Can you give me a receipt? | ¿Puede darme un recibo?<br>PWEH-deh DAR-meh oon reh-SEEboh |
| I think this is wrong. | Creo que esto está mal.<br>KREH-oh KEH ES-toh es-TAH mal |
| Can I have... | ¿Puedo tener...<br>PWEH-doh teh-NEHR |
| ...a lead apron? | ...un delantal de plomo?<br>oon deh-lanTAL deh PLOH-moh |

| | |
|---|---|
| How long will this examination take? | ¿Cuánto tiempo tomará este estudio?<br>KWAN-toh teeEM-poh toh-MAHrah ES-teh esTOO-deeoh |
| What room is my father in? | ¿En qué cuarto es mi padre?<br>en KEH QWAR-toh es mee PAH-dreh |

\* -o- for the masculine and -a- for the feminine

*Spanish for Radiology Professionals*

# POSSIBLE ANSWERS OR DIRECTIONS

| | |
|---|---|
| Yes, certainly. | Sí, por supuesto.<br>see, pohr soo-poo-EStoh |
| Sorry. | Lo siento.<br>loh seeEN-toh |
| I don't think so. | Creo que no.<br>KREH-oh keh noh |
| I think so. | Yo creo.<br>joh KREH-oh |
| The bathroom is occupied now. | El cuarto de baño es ocupado ahora.<br>El QWAR-toh deh BAH-nyoh es ohkoo-PAHdoh ah-OHrah |
| Ask at... | Pregunte en ...<br>pre-GOONteh en |
| ...the information desk. | ...la mesa de información.<br>lah MEH-sah deh een-for-mah-SEEON |
| ...the reception desk. | ...la mesa de recepción.<br>lah MEH-sah deh reh-sepSEEON |
| No. The public telephone is... | No. El teléfono público es...<br>noh. el tehLEH-foh-noh POOBleek-oh es |
| ...in the emergency room. | ...en la sala de emergéncia<br>en lah SAH-lah deh eh-mer-HENsee-ah |
| ...on the first floor. | ...en el primer piso.<br>en el pree-MEHR PEE-soh |
| ...in the basement. | ...en el sótano<br>en el SOHtah-noh |
| ...by the lab. | ...cerca del laboratorio.<br>SER-kah del lah-boh-rah-TOHree-oh |
| Through here/there. | Por aquí / allá.<br>pohr ah-KEE /ah-JAH |
| Over here/there. | Aquí /allá.<br>ah-KEE /ah-JAH |

| | |
|---|---|
| Go straight. | Vaya directamente.<br>BAH-jah deh-rehtahMENteh |
| Make a right/left. | Haga un derecho/una izquierda.<br>AHgah oon deh-REHchah/oona ees-KEYEERdah |
| ...then a right/left. | Luego a la derecha/a la izquierda.<br>looEH-goh ah lah deh-REHchah/ ah lah ees-KEYEERdah |
| Turn right/left. | Gire a la derecha /a lah izquierda.<br>GEE-reh ah lah deh-REHchah/ ah lah ees-KEYEERdah |
| Take the next right. | Tome la próxima a la derecha.<br>TOH-meh lah PROKsee-mah ah lah deh-REHcha |
| Take the first left.. | Tome la primera izquierda...<br>TOH-meh lah pree-MEHrah ees-KEYEERdah |
| ...the second right. | ...el segundo derecho<br>El seh-GOONdah deh-REHchah |
| Turn right after you pass the door. | Gire a la derecha después de que usted pase la puerta.<br>GEE-reh ah la deh-REHchah dehs-POOES deh KEH oosTED PAH-seh lah PWER-tah |
| ...after you pass the... | ...después de que pase...<br>dehs-POOES deh KEH PAH-seh... |
| ...elevators. | ...las ascensores.<br>las as-sen-SOHres |
| ...information desk. | ...la mesa de información.<br>lah MEH-sah deh een-for-mah-SEEON |
| ...stairs. | ...las escaleras.<br>las es-kah-LEHras |
| At these/those doors. | En estas/aquellas puertas.<br>en es-TAH /ah-KEjas PWER-tas |

## *Spanish for Radiology Professionals*

| | |
|---|---|
| At the stairs. | En las escaleras.<br>en las es-kah-LEHras |
| At the water fountain. | En la fuente de agua.<br>en lah foo-ENteh deh AH-gwah |
| It is not far/near. | No esta lejos/cerca.<br>noh es-TAH LEH-hos/SER-kah |
| It is not far/it is not near. | No es distante/ no está cerca.<br>noh es deesTANteh/noh es-TAH SER-kah |
| It is far/it is near. | Es distante/ está cerca.<br>es deesTANteh es-TAH SER-kah |
| On your (the) right/left. | A la derecha/izquierda.<br>ah lah deh-REHchah/ ees-KEYEERdah |
| First/last/next. | Primer/último/próximo.<br>pree-MEHR/OOLtee-moh/PROKsee-moh |
| Opposite/behind. | Enfrente/atrás.<br>enFREN-teh/ah-TRAS |
| Next to/after... | Junto a/después de...<br>JOON-toh ah/dehs-POOES deh |
| Your father is in room number five zero one. (501) | Su padre está en el cuarto cinco-cero uno.<br>Soo PAH-dreh esTAH en el QWAR-toh SEEN-koh SEH-roh oona |

# PROBLEMS AND EMERGENCIES

## GENERAL QUESTIONS AND EXPRESSIONS

| | |
|---|---|
| Can you get me a doctor? | ¿Puede llamar a un doctor?<br>PWEH-deh jah-MAHR ah oon dohk-TOHR |
| I need a doctor, quickly. | Necesito un doctor, pronto.<br>neh-seh-SEEtoh oon dohk-TOHR, PRON-toh |
| I am pregnant. | Estoy embarazada.<br>es-TOY em-bah-rah-SAHdah |
| I have a heart problem. | Tengo problemas de corazón.<br>TEHN-goh proh-BLEMas deh koh-rahSON |
| I have a pain in my chest. | Tengo un dolor en el pecho.<br>TEHN-goh oon doh-LOHR en el PEH-choh |
| I have difficulty breathing. | Tengo dificultad respirando.<br>TEHN-goh dee-fee-koolTAHD rehs-pee-RAN-doh |
| I am allergic to... | Soy alérgico/a a ...   *<br>soh-ee ALEHRgee-koh/ah ah |
| ...penicillin. | ...la penicilina.<br>lah peh-nee-see-LEEnah |
| I am ...diabetic. | Soy...diabético/a   *<br>soh-ee...deeah-BEHtee-koh |
| ...asthmatic. | ...asmático/a.   *<br>ahs-MAHtee-koh/ah |
| I have... hemorrhoids. | Tengo... hemorroides.<br>TEHN-goh...ehm-moh-ROHEE-des |
| ...rheumatism. | ...reumatismo.<br>reh-oo-mah-TEESmoh |
| ...diarrhea. | ...diarrea.<br>dee-ah-REHah |

## *Spanish for Radiology Professionals*

| | |
|---|---|
| At what time does the doctor leave? | ¿A qué hora se va el doctor?<br>ah KEH OH-rah seh vah el dohk-TOHR |
| Can I have... | ¿Puede darme...<br>PWEH-deh DAR-meh... |
| ...an aspirin? | ...una aspirina?<br>OOna as-peer-REEnah |
| ...a pain killer? | ...un analgésico?<br>oon ah-nal-GEHsee-koh |
| ...a sedative/tranquillizer? | ...un sedativo?<br>oon seh-dahTEE-boh |
| ...some facial tissue? | ...papel faciál?<br>pah-PEHL fah-seeAL |
| ...some toilet paper? | ...papel de excusado/papel higiénico?<br>pah-PEHL deh eks-kooSAH-doh/pah-PEHL eeAYN-nee-koh |
| ...a sanitary napkin? | ...una toalla sanitaria?<br>OOna toh-AHjas san-eeTAH-reeah |
| ...some tampons? | ...unos tampones (higienicos)?<br>OOnos tamPOHN-ehs (eeAYN-nee-koh) |
| ...some water? | ...agua?<br>AH-gwah |
| I have broken... | Se me han roto...<br>seh meh ahn ROH-toh |
| ...my glasses. | ...los lentes.<br>los LEN-tehs |
| ...my denture. | ...la dentadura.<br>lah den-tah-DOOrah |
| I have lost ... | He perdido...<br>heh per-DEEdoh |
| ...my contact lens. | ...los lentes de contacto/ laslentillas.<br>los LEN-tehs deh kon-TAHKtoh/las len-TEEyas |

| | |
|---|---|
| ...my handbag/pocket book. | ...la cartera.<br>lah kar-TEHrah |
| ...my jewelry. | ...la joyeria.<br>lah hoh-jehREEah |
| ...my keys. | ...las llaves.<br>las JAH-behs |
| ...my necklace. | ...el collar.<br>el koh-JAHR |
| ...my ring. | ...la sortija.<br>lah sor-TEEhah |
| ...my wallet. | ...el monedero.<br>el moh-neh-DEHroh |
| ...my watch. | ...el reloj de pulsera.<br>el reh-LOH deh pool-SEHRrah |
| ...my x-ray request. | ...mi orden de rayos x.<br>mee ohr-DEHN deh RAH-jos EH-kees |
| I am lost. | Me he perdido.<br>meh heh per-DEEdoh |
| I want to leave at 2 o'clock. | Yo quiero salir a las dos.<br>joh KEE-EHroh sah-LEER ah las dohs |
| I have been here for one hour. | Estoy aquí hace una hora.<br>es-TOY ah-KEE AH-seh OOna OH-rah |
| I need something for the pain. | Necesito algo para el dolor.<br>neh-sehSEEtoh ALgoh PAHrah el dohLOR |
| I need.../I'd like... | Necesito.../Quiero...<br>neh-seh-SEEtoh.../KEE-EHroh |
| I am in pain. | Me duele.<br>meh DWEH-leh |
| I've had this pain for.. | He estado con este dolor...<br>eh es-TAHdoh kon ES-teh doh-LOHR |
| ...one hour/one day. | ...una hora/un día.<br>OOna OH-rah/ oon DEEah |

## *Spanish for Radiology Professionals*

| | |
|---|---|
| ...two hours/two days. | ...dos horas/dos días.<br>dohs OHR-ahs / dos DEE-ahs |
| I have a pain in my... | Tengo un dolor en el/la<br>TEHN-goh oon doh-LOHR en el/lah... |
| It is a...sharp pain. | Es un... dolor intenso.<br>es doh-LOHR een-TENsoh |
| ...a dull ache. | ...dolor sordo.<br>doh-LOHR SOHR-doh |
| ...nagging pain/continuous. | ...dolor continuo.<br>doh-LOHR kohn-TEEnoo-oh |
| My chest hurts. | Me duele el pecho.<br>meh DWEH-leh el PEH-choh |
| My head hurts | Me duele la cabeza<br>meh DWEH-leh lah cahBEHsah |
| There/here hurts. | Allá/aquí me duele.<br>ah-JAH/ah-KEE meh DWEH-leh |
| It hurts...a lot. | Me duele...mucho.<br>meh DWEH-leh ...MOO-choh |
| ...most of the time. | ...casi todo el tiempo.<br>KAHsee TOH-doh el teeEM-poh |
| My child is ill. | Mi hijo/a está enfermo. *<br>mee EE-hoh/hah es-TAH en-FEHRmoh |
| I am ill. | Estoy enfermo/a. *<br>es-TOY en-FEHRmoh/ah |
| I feel...ill. | Me siento ...enfermo/a. *<br>meh seeEN-toh ...en-FEHRmoh/ah |
| ...faint/weak. | ...débil.<br>DEH-beel |
| ...feverish. | ...febril.<br>feh-BREEL |
| ...nauseous/sick. | ...náuseas.<br>NAWseh-ahs |

| | |
|---|---|
| ...dizzy. | ...mareado/a. * |
| | mah-reh-AHdoh/ah |
| | |
| I am dizzy. | Estoy mareado. |
| | es-TOY mah-reh-AHdoh |
| | |
| I am going to faint. | Me voy a desmayar. |
| | meh boy ah des-mahJAHR |
| | |
| I would like...please. | Me gustaría... por favor. |
| | meh goos-tarREE-ah...pohr fah-BOHR |
| | |
| ...something for this cold... | ...algo para el catarro... |
| | AL-goh PAH-rah el kah-TAHroh |
| | |
| ...something for the flu... | ...algo para gripe... |
| | AL-goh PAH-rah GREE-peh |
| | |
| I am fine now. | Me siento bien ahora. |
| | meh seeEN-toh beeEN ah-OHrah |
| | |
| Please can I have...? | ¿Por favor podría tener...? |
| | pohr fah-BOHR poh-DREEah ten-EHR |

\* Use -o- for the masculine and -a- for the femine.

*Spanish for Radiology Professionals*

# RELATED QUESTIONS AND REPLIES

| | |
|---|---|
| Are you... | ¿Está usted...<br>es-TAH oosTED |
| ...taking any medicine? | ...tomando algun medicina?<br>toh-MANdoh AHL-goon meh-dee-SEEnah |
| ...pregnant? | ...embarazada?<br>em-bahrah-SAHdah |
| ...allergic to any medication? | ...alérgico a algún medicamento?<br>ah-LERgee-koh ah ahl-GOON meh-dee-kah-MENtoh |
| ...asthmatic? | ...asmático/a?  \*<br>as-MAHtee-koh/ah |
| ...diabetic? | ...diabético/a?  \*<br>deeah-BEHtee-koh/ah |
| ...on insulin? | ...en insulina?<br>en een-soo-LEEnah |
| Do you take insulin? | ¿Toma usted insulina?<br>TOH-mah oosTED een-soo-LEEnah |
| Did you take your insulin? | ¿Tomó usted la insulina?<br>toh-MOH oosTED lah een-soo-LEEnah |
| Do you have a heart problem? | ¿Tiene algún problema del corazon?<br>teeEN-eh ahl-GOON proh-BLEMah del koh-rahSON |
| Can I get you...some water? | ¿Le puedo dar...aqua?<br>leh PWEH-doh dar  AH-gwah |
| ...something to drink? | ...algo de beber?<br>...ALgoh deh BEHbehr |
| ...something to eat? | ...algo de comer?<br>ALgoh deh koh-MER |
| ...something sweets? | ...algo dulce?<br>ALgoh DOOL-seh |

63

| | |
|---|---|
| ...a chair? | ...una silla?<br>oona SEE-jah |
| Please lie down over here. | Acuéstese aquí, por favor.<br>ah-kooES-teh-seh ah-KEE, pohr fah-BOHR |
| Please write down all medicine that you are taking. | Por favor escriba todo medicina que está tomando.<br>pohr fah-BOHR es-KREEbah TOH-doh meh-dee-SEEnah keh esTAH toh-MANdoh |
| Please write it down. | Por favor escribalo.<br>pohr fah-BOHR es-kree-BAHloh |
| What medicine are you allergic to? | ¿Qué medicina es usted alérgico?<br>keh meh-dee-SEEnah es oosTED ah-LERgee-koh |
| Where does it hurt? | ¿Dónde le duele?<br>DON-deh leh DWEL-eh |
| Does it hurt here?(point) | ¿El dolor es aquí?<br>el doh-LOHR es ah-KEE |
| Take this now. | Tome esto ahora.<br>TOH-meh EStoh ah-OHrah |
| Sit down here. | Siéntese aquí.<br>see-ENteh-seh...ah-KEE |
| Lie down. | Acuéstese.<br>ah-KOOESteh-seh |
| Breathe deeply. | Respire profundo.<br>res-PEEreh pro-FOONdoh |
| Breathe through your mouth. | Coja aire por la boca.<br>KOH-hah AY-reh pohr lah BOH-kah |
| Take a big breath and hold it. | Respira profundo y aguántalo.<br>res-PEErah proh-FOONdoh ee ah-GWANtah-loh |
| Please take a big breath. | Por favor tómese un respiro grande.<br>Poh fahVOHR TOHmeh-seh oon rehsPEEroh GRAH-deh |

## *Spanish for Radiology Professionals* 65

| | |
|---|---|
| Open your mouth. | Abra la boca. <br> AH-brah lah BOH-kah |
| Cough please. | Tosa, por favor. <br> TOH-sah, pohr fah-BOHR |
| Come with me. | Venga conmigo. <br> BEN-gah kon-MEEgoh |
| Follow me. | Sígame. <br> SEEgah-meh |
| Wait here. | Espere aquí. <br> es-PEHreh ah-KEE |
| I'm sorry, but I can't help you. | Lo siento, pero no puedo ayudarle. <br> loh seeEN-TOH, PEH-roh noh PWEH-doh ah-joo-DARleh |
| The nurse/doctor will take your blood pressure/temperature. | La enfermera/el doctor va a tomar la presión/ la temperatura. <br> lah en-fehr-MEHrah /el dohk-TOHR bah ah toh-MAR lah preh-SEEON/ lah tem-pehrah-TOOrah |
| I will get the doctor. | Voy a illamar al doctor/medico <br> BOH ah eeYAHmar al dohk-TOHR/ mehDEEkoh |
| I will get the doctor. | Yo podría conseguir al doctor. <br> joh poh-DREEah kon-sehGEER al dohk-TOHR |
| You must fill this prescription today. | (Usted) Debe conseguir esta prescripcion hoy. <br> (oosTED)DEH-beh kon-seeGEER EStah prehs-creep-SEEON oi |
| Take...teaspoons of this medicine. | Tome...cucharillas de esta medicina. <br> TOH-meh...koo-chah-REEjas deh ES-tah meh-dee-SEEnah |
| Take this/these pills... | Tome esta/estas píldora/s <br> TOH-meh ES-tah/ES-tas PEEL-doh-rah/as |

| | |
|---|---|
| ...with a glass of water. | con un vaso de agua.<br>kon oon BAH-soh deh AH-gwah |
| ...tonight. | ...noche.<br>NOH-cheh |
| ...now. | ...ahora.<br>ah-OHrah |
| ...every hour. | ...cada hora.<br>KAH-dah OH-rah |
| ...every...hours. | ...cada...horas.<br>KAH-dah...OH-ras |
| ...twice /4 times a day. | ...dos/cuatro veces al día.<br>dos/KWAH-troh BEH-sehs al DEEah |
| ...before/after each meal. | ...antes/después de cada comida.<br>AN-tes/deh-POOES deh KAH-dah koh-MEEdah |
| ...in the morning/at night. | ...por la mañana/ por la noche.<br>pohr lah mah-NYAHnah/ pohr lah NOH-cheh |
| ...in case of pain. | ...en caso de dolor.<br>en KAH-soh deh doh-LOR |
| ...for four days. | ...durante cuatro días.<br>doo-RANteh KWAH-troh DEE-as |

*Use -o- for the masculine and -a- for the feminine.

# -Usted- can be omitted.

*Spanish for Radiology Professionals* 67

# FILLING OUT FORMS

## GENERAL QUESTIONS AND EXPRESSIONS

What is your name?  ¿Cómo se llama?
KOH-moh seh JAH-mah

Have you had previous x-rays here?  ¿Ha tenido aquí radiografías anteriormente?
ah teh-NEEdoh ah-KEE rah-deeoh-grah-FEEas an-teh-reeohr-MEHNteh

...an Ultrasound?  ...un ultrasonido?
oon ool-trah-soh-NEEdoh

...an M.R.I?  ...una resonancia magnética?
OOnah rehsoh-NAN-seeah magNEH-teekah

When?  ¿Cuándo?
KWAN-doh

Where were your x-rays taken?  ¿En dónde le tomaron los radiografías (los placas)?                #
en DON-deh leh toh-MAHron las rah-deeoh-grah-FEEas (las PLAH-kas)

What is your age?  ¿Cuál es su edad?
kwal es soo eh-DAD

Are you pregnant?  ¿Está usted embarazada?
es-TAH oosTED em-bah-rah-SAHdah

What is your...  ¿Cuál es su...
kwal es soo...

...address?  ...dirección?
dee-rek-SEEON

...name?  ...nombre?
NOHM-breh

...your spouse's name?  ...nombre de su esposo/a?                *
NOHM-breh deh soo esPOH-soh/sah

...doctor's name?  ...nombre de su doctor?
NOHM-breh deh soo dohk-TOHR

| | |
|---|---|
| ...last name? | ...apellido?<br>ah-peh-JEEdoh |
| ...first name? | ...primer nombre?<br>pree-MEHR NOHN-breh |
| ...maiden name? | ...nombre de soltera?<br>NOHM-bre deh sohl-TEHrah |
| ...place of birth? | ...lugar de nacimiento?<br>loo-GAHR deh nah-see-meeEN-toh |
| ...date of birth? | ...fecha de nacimiento?<br>FEH-cha deh nah-see-meeEN-toh |
| ...business number? | ...número del trabajo?<br>NOOmeh-roh del trah-BAHoh |
| ...home phone number? | ...número de la casa?<br>NOOmeh-roh deh lah KAH-sah |
| ...social security number? | ...número de seguro social?<br>NOOmeh-roh deh seh-GOOroh soh-seeAL |
| ...business address? | ...dirección del trabajo?<br>dee-rek-SEEON del trah-BAHoh |
| ...work address? | ...dirección del trabajo de su..<br>dee-rek-SEEON del trah-BAH-joh deh soo.. |
| ...occupation? | ...ocupación?<br>oh-koo-pah-SEEON |
| ...zip code? | ...zona postal?<br>SOHnah pohs-TAHL |
| ...City and State? | ...ciudad y estado?<br>see-ooDAD ee esTAH-doh. |
| What is the...? | ¿Cuál es el...?<br>kwal es el |
| ...your spouse. | ...esposo/a?         *<br>soo esPOH-soh/sah |
| Where do you work? | ¿Dónde usted trabaja?<br>DON-deh OOSted trah-BAHhah |

## *Spanish for Radiology Professionals*

| | |
|---|---|
| What is your health insurance number? | ¿Cuál es su número de su seguro medico?<br>kwal es soo NOOmeh-roh deh soo seh-GOOroh MEHdee-coh |
| May I see your health insurance card? | ¿Puedo ver su tarjeta de seguro médico?<br>PWEH-doh ber soo tar-HEHtah deh seh-GOOroh MEHdee-coh |
| Do you have... | ¿Tiene usted...<br>teeEN-eh oosTED |
| ...health insurance? | ...seguro médica?<br>seh-GOO-roh MEHdee-kah |
| ...any children? | ...hijos?<br>EE-hos |
| How many children do you have? | ¿Cuántos hijos tiene?<br>KWAN-tos EE-hos teeEN-eh |
| Are you married? | ¿Es usted casado/a?                                    *<br>es oosTED kah-SAHdoh/ah |
| What is the name of your family doctor? | ¿Cuál es el nombre de su médico de familia?<br>kwal es el NOHM-breh deh soo MEHdee-coh deh fahMEELeeah |
| Please... | Por favor...<br>pohr fah-BOHR... |
| ...fill out this form. | ...llene este formulario.<br>JEH-neh ES-teh fohr-moo-LAHreeoh |
| ...sign here. | ...firme aquí.<br>FEER-meh ah-KEE |
| ...take this to the billing department. | ...lleve esto al departamento de cobro.<br>JEH-beh ES-toh al deh-partah-MENtoh deh KOHB-roh |
| ...write here. | ...escríbalo aquí.<br>es-KREEBAH-loh ah-KEE |
| ...write your name here. | ...escriba su nombre aquí.<br>es-KREEbah soo NOHM-breh ah-KEE |

# RELATED REPLIES

| | |
|---|---|
| My name is... | Mi nombre es.../Me llamo...<br>mee NOHM-breh es.../meh JAH-moh... |
| I am... | (Yo) soy...<br>(joh) soh-ee |
| ...married. | ...casado/a. *<br>kah-SAHdoh/ah |
| ...single. | ...soltero/a. *<br>sohl-TEHroh/ah |
| ...widowed. | ...viudo/a. *<br>BEE-OOdoh |
| ...divorced. | ...divorciado/a. *<br>dee-bor-SEE-AHdoh/ah |
| I have... | (Yo) tengo...<br>(joh) TEHN-goh |
| ...one daughter. | ...una hija<br>OOnah EE-hah |
| ...one son. | ...un hijo.<br>oon EE-hoh |
| ...two daughters/sons. | ...dos hijas/hijos.<br>dos EE-has/EE-hos |
| I don't have any children. | No tengo hijos/as.<br>noh TEHN-goh EE-hos/as |
| I am pregnant. | Estoy embarazanda.<br>es-TOY em-bah-rah-SAHdah |
| I am a student. | Soy estudiante.<br>soh-ee es-too-DEE-ANteh |

\# The word -placa- is commonly used to refer to an x-ray. The correct Spanish word is radiografía.
\* Use -o- for the masculine and -a- for the femine.

# PATIENT CARE

## GENERAL QUESTIONS

| | |
|---|---|
| Come this way. | Venga acá.<br>BEN-gah ah-KAH |
| You cannot have any... | Usted no puede tomar...<br>oos-TED noh pweh-deh to-MAR |
| ...liquids. | ...líquidos.<br>LEEkee-doh |
| ...water. | ...agua.<br>AH-gwah |
| ...food. | comida.<br>koh-MEEdah |
| You cannot eat anything. | No puede comer nada.<br>noh PWEH-deh koh-MER NAHdah |
| You can have only ice chips. | Puede comer sólo hielo.<br>PWEH-deh koh-MER SOHloh YEEHloh |
| Relax, the test will be over... | Tranquiliseze, el estudio se terminará...<br>trahn-kee-LEEsee-seh el es- TOOdee-oh se ter-mee-nahRAH |
| ...soon. | ...pronto.<br>PRON-toh |
| ...in half an hour. | ...en media hora.<br>en meh-DEEah OH-rah |
| You will have to lie on this table... | Usted tendra que acostarse en esta mesa...<br>oosTED TEHN-drah keh ah-kohs-TAHRseh en ES-tah MEH-sah |
| ...for half an hour. | ...media hora.<br>meh-DEEah OH-rah |
| ...during the study. | ...durante el estudio.<br>doo-RANteh el es-TOOdee-oh |

| | |
|---|---|
| Let me help you. | Dejeme ayudarle.<br>DEH-heh-meh ah-joo-DARleh |
| Do not remove... | No remueva...<br>noh reh-MOOEH-bah |
| ...the bandage. | ...el vendaje.<br>el ben-DAHheh |
| Where does it hurt? | ¿Dónde le duele?<br>DON-deh le DWEL-eh |
| Does it hurt here? (point) | ¿Le duele aquí?<br>le DWEL-eh ah-KEE |
| Did you hurt your hand? | ¿Le duele la mano?<br>le DWEL-eh lah MAH-noh |
| I want to examine you. | Quiero examinarlo.<br>kee-EERoh ek-ahmee-NARloh |
| Please sit up on the bed. | Por favor siéntese en la cama.<br>por fah-BOHR seeEN-tehseh en la KAH-mah |
| Can you move over onto the bed? | ¿Puede moverse hacia la cama?<br>PWEH-deh moh-BERseh hSEEah lah KAH-mah |
| I am going to take your temperature. | Voy a tomarle la temperatura.<br>boy ah toh-MARleh lah tem-peh-rahTOOrah |
| Open your mouth. | Abra la boca.<br>AH-brah lah BOH-kah |
| Lift up your tongue. | Suba la lengua.<br>SOO-bah lah LEN-gwah |
| Keep your mouth closed. | No abra la boca.<br>noh AH-brah lah BOH-kah |
| Please keep still. | Por favor no se mueva.<br>pohr fah-BOHR noh seh MWEH-bah |
| Extend your arm. | Extienda su brazo.<br>ekTEE-ENdah soo BRAH-soh |

## *Spanish for Radiology Professionals*

| | |
|---|---|
| Roll up...please. | Enrolle...por favor. |
| | en-ROHjeh...pohr fab-BOHR |
| ...your sleeves... | ...la manga... |
| | lah MAHN-gah |
| ...the sleeves of your blouse... | ...la manga de la blusa. |
| | lah MAHN-gah deh lah BLOO-sah |
| Let me check your... | Voy a verificar su... |
| | boy ah beh-ree-feeKAR soo |
| ...pulse. | ...pulso. |
| | POOLsoh |
| ...I.V.(intravenous) | ...intravenosa. |
| | een-trah-behNOHsah |
| ...vein. | ...vena. |
| | BEHnah |
| This will be... | Esto será ... |
| | ES-toh sehRAH |
| ...cold. | ...frío. |
| | FREEoh |
| ...hot. | ...caliente. |
| | kah-LEE-ENteh |
| ...hard. | ...duro. |
| | DOOroh |
| ...soft. | ...suave. |
| | SWAHbeh |
| I am going to remove... | Voy a remover ... |
| | boy ah reh-mohBER |
| ...the bandage. | ...la venda/curita. |
| | lah BENdah/koo-REEtah |
| ...the dressing. | ...el vendaje. |
| | el benDAH-heh |
| ...these stitches. | ...estos puntos. |
| | EStos POON-tos |

| | |
|---|---|
| ...the sutures. | ...las suturas.<br>las sooTOO-ras |
| Can I get you something for the pain? | ¿Podría tener algo para este dolor?<br>pohDREE-ah teh-NER ALgoh PAHrah ESteh doh-LOHR |
| These are for the pain. | Estos son para el dolor.<br>EStos son PAH-rah el doh-LOHR |
| Take two of these. | Tome dos de estos.<br>TOH-meh dos deh EStos |
| Are you allergic to any medication? | Es usted alérgico a algún medicamento.<br>es oosTED ah-LERgee-koh ah ahl-GOON meh-dee-kahMENtoh |
| Are you still feeling pain? | ¿Toda vía le duele?<br>TOHdah BEEah leh DWEH-leh |
| All your test were negative. | Todo el estudio es negativo.<br>TOHdoh el es-TOOdee-oh es neh-gah-TEEboh |
| It is not serious. | No es grave.<br>noh es GRAH-beh |
| Ask the doctor for the results of your tests. | Pregunte al doctor el resultado del estudio.<br>preh-GOONteh al dohk-TOHR el reh-soolTAH-doh del es-TOOdee-oh |
| Everything is normal. | Todo está normal.<br>TOHdoh esTAH nohr-MAL |
| The doctor has not yet arrived. | El doctor todavía no ha llegado.<br>El dohk-TOHR tohdahBEEAH noh hah yeh-GAHdoh |
| I will get someone who speaks Spanish | Buscare alguien que hable español.<br>boos-KAH-reh AHL-giehn keh AHB-leh es-pah-NYOL |
| I'm the nurse. | Soy el enfermero.<br>soh-ee el ehn-fehrMEHroh |

## Spanish for Radiology Professionals

| | |
|---|---|
| I am the x-ray technologist. | (Yo) Soy... el técnico radiográfica -OR- ... el tecnólogo de rayos X.   # (joh) soy el TEKnee-koh rah-dee-oh-GRAHfee-kah/ el tekNOH-loh-goh de RAH-ohs eh-KES |
| Do not touch that electrical cable. | No toques ese cable eléctrico. Noh TOH-keh EH-seh KAHB-leh ehLEHC-tree-koh |
| You cannot... | No puede ... noh PWEH-deh |
| ...get out of bed today. | ...levantárse de la cama hoy leh-ban-TARseh deh lah KAH-mah oi |
| ...take a bath today. | ... bañarse hoy. bah-NYARseh oi |
| Do not try to sit up. | No tráte de levantárse. noh TRAH-teh deh leh-banTAR-seh |
| You must... | Tiene que ... teeEN-eh keh |
| ...get out of bed today. | ...levantárse de la cama hoy. leh-ban-TARseh deh lah KAH-mah oi |
| ...try to sit up. | ... tratar de sentarse. trah-TAHR deh senTAR-seh |
| ...get up and walk today. | ...levantárse y caminar hoy. leh-ban-TARseh ee kah-meeNAR oi |
| ...sit in the chair today. | ...sentarse en la silla hoy. sen-TAHRseh en lah SEEL-lah oi |
| You can only have a shower. | Solo puedo ducharse. SOH-loh PWEH-doh dooCHAR-seh |
| Do not bathe for... | No se bañe por... noh seh BAH-nyeh pohr |
| Do not take a bath until this wound heals. | No se bañe hasta que la herida sane. noh seh BAH-nyeh AHS-tah keh lah eh-REEdah SAH-neh |

| | |
|---|---|
| You are going to have an x-ray today. | Va a tener unos rayos equis hoy. bah ah tehn-NER OOnos RAH-jos EH-kees oi |
| You may get some bleeding for a few days. | Tal vez va a sangrar por par de días. tal bes vah ah sahn-GRAR por par deh DEE-as |
| Do not put anything into your vagina for... | No ponga nada en su vagína por... noh POHN-gah NAH-dah en soo bah-GEEnah por |
| no douche | no ducha noh DOO-chah |
| no sex. | no sexo. noh SEK-so |
| no tampons. | no tampones. noh tam-POHN-ehs |
| I need a sample of your blood/stools/urine. | Necesito una muestra de sangre/heces/orina. neh-sehSEEtoh OOnah MWEHS-trah deh SAHN-greh/EH-sehs/ ohREEnah |

\* Use –o- for the maculine and –a- for the feminine

# The pronoun can be omitted.

# POSSIBLE RESPONSES

| | |
|---|---|
| I cannot eat/sleep. | Yo no puedo comer/dormir.<br>joh noh PWEH-doh koh-MER/dohr-MEER |
| I need sleeping pills. | Necesito pildoras para dormir.<br>neh-sehSEEtoh peel-DOHras PAH-rah dohr-MEER |
| I am allergic to peninsulin. | Soy alégico a penisilina.<br>soh-ee ah-LEHgee-koh ah peh-nee seeLEEnah |
| It hurts here. | Duele aquí.<br>DWEH-leh ah-KEE |
| I cannot turn. | No puedo virarme.<br>noh PWEH-doh beeRAHR-meh |
| I cannot move. | No puedo mover.<br>noh PWEH-doh moh-BER |
| ...my neck. | ...mi cuello.<br>mee KWEH-joh |
| ...my leg. | ...mi pierna.<br>mee PEE-ERnah |
| I cannot lift my leg. | No puedo levantar mi pierna.<br>noh PWEH-doh leh-banTAR mee PEE-ERnah |
| Is it broken? | ¿Está rota?<br>esTAH ROH-tah |
| I need ... | Necesito<br>neh-seh-SEEtoh |
| ...washbasin. | ... una palangana.<br>OOnah pah-lan-GAHnah |
| ...a bedpan. | ...una silleta.<br>OOnah seel-LEHtah |
| I want to comb my hair. | Quiero peinarme.<br>kee-EERoh pej-NARmeh |

| | |
|---|---|
| When can I get up? | ¿Cuándo puedo levantarme?<br>QWAN-doh PWEH-doh leh-ban-TARmeh |
| When can I go home? | ¿Cuándo puedo írme a casa?<br>QWAN-doh PWEH-doh EER-meh ah KAH-sah |
| What are the visiting hours? | ¿Cuáles son las horas de visita?<br>KWAH-les son las OH-ras de beeSEE-tah |
| Can I go home tomorrow? | ¿Puedo írme a casa mañana?<br>PWEH-doh EERmeh ah KAH-sah mah-NYAHnah |
| What time can the doctor come? | ¿A qué hora puede venir el doctor?<br>ah keh OH-rah PWEH-deh beh-NEER el dohk-TOHR |
| I want to speak to the doctor. | Quiero hablar con el doctor.<br>kee-EERoh ahb-LAR kon el dohk-TOHR |
| I must call... | Tengo que llamar a...<br>TEHN-goh keh jah-MAHR ah |
| ...my husband/wife. | ...mi esposo/a.  \*<br>mee esPOH-soh/sah |
| ...my sister/brother. | ...mi hermana/o.<br>mee erMAH-nah/noh |

\* Use -o- for the masculine and -a- for the feminine.

## *Spanish for Radiology Professionals*

# UNDRESSING THE PATIENT

| | |
|---|---|
| The changing room is... | El cuarto de cambiarse es... <br> el QWAR-toh deh cam-BEEAR-seh es... |
| ...this way. | ...en este lado. <br> en ES-teh LAD-doh |
| ...over there. | ...allá. <br> ah-JAH |
| ...over here. | ...aquí. <br> ah-KEE |
| Remove your clothes please. | Desvístase, por favor. <br> des-BEEStah-seh, pohr fah-BOHR |
| Please remove all your clothes and put this gown on. | Por favor, quítese todo la ropa y coloquese esta bata. <br> pohr fah-BOHR, KEEteh-seh TOH-doh lah ROH-pah ee koh-LOHkeh-seh ES-tah BAH-tah |
| Put the opening... | Colóquese la parte... <br> koh-LOHkeh-seh lah PAR-teh... |
| ... to the back. | ...hacia atrás. <br> AH-seeah ah-TRAS |
| ...to the front. | ...hacia el frente. <br> AH-seeah el FREN-teh |
| Undress to the waist. | Quítese la ropa hasta la cintura. <br> KEEteh-seh lah ROH-pah as-tah lah sen-TOOrah |
| Undress... | Quitese la ropa... <br> KEEteh-seh lah ROH-pah |
| ...from the waist up. | ...de la cintura para arríba. <br> deh lah sen-TOOrah PAH-rah ah-REEbah |
| ...from the waist down. | ...de la cintura para abajo. <br> deh lah sen-TOOrah PAH-rah ah-BAHoh |
| Undress... | Desvístase... <br> dehs-BEEStah-seh |

| | |
|---|---|
| ...here. | ...aquí.<br>ah-KEE |
| ...there. | ...allá<br>ah-JAH |
| Are you wearing... | ¿Está usted usando...<br>es-TAH oosTED ooSAN-doh... |
| ...any jewelry? | ...alguna prenda?<br>ahl-GOONah PREN-dah |
| ...anything with buttons? | ...algo con botones?<br>AHL-goh con boh-TOHnes |
| ...anything with pins. | ...algo con pinche?<br>AHL-goh con PEEN-cheh |
| ...a bra? | ...un sostén -or- brassier?<br>oon soos-TEN/bras-SEEey |
| Please remove... | Por favor remueva...<br>pohr fah-BOHR reh-MOOEH-bah |
| ...your earring. | ...las pantallas.<br>las pan-TAHyas |
| ...your chains. | ...las cadenas.<br>las kah-DEHnas |
| ...your hair pins/clips. | ...las pinches de pelo.<br>las PEEN-chez deh PEH-loh |
| ...your ring. | ...la sortija.<br>lah sor-TEEhah |
| ...your watch. | ...el reloj.<br>el reh-LOH |
| ...your bracelet. | ...la pulsera.<br>lah pool-SEHrah |
| Please remove everything from your pockets. | Por favor, remueva todo de los bolsillos.<br>pohr fah-BOHR reh-MOOEH-bah TOH-doh deh los bol-SEE-jos |
| Do you have anything in your pockets? | ¿Usted tiene algo en los bolsillos?<br>oosTED teeEN-eh AHL-goh en los bol-SEE-jos |

## *Spanish for Radiology Professionals*

| | |
|---|---|
| Do not tie the string of the gown. | No se amarre los tirantes de la bata.<br>noh seh ah-MARR-reh los tee-RAHN-tehs deh lah BAH-tah |
| Please untie the strings of the gown. | Por favor sueltese los tirantes de la bata.<br>pohr fah-BOHR swel-TEH-seh los tee-RAHN-tehs deh lah BAH-tah |
| Are you wearing a bra? | ¿Tiene el sostén puesto?<br>teeEN-eh el soos-TEN PWES-toh |
| Please attach the st raps of the gown. | Ate por favor los tirantes de la bata.<br>AH-teh pohr-fah-BOHR los teeRAHN-tehs deh lah BAH-tah |
| Take...off. | Quítese...<br>KEEteh-seh |
| ...your bra... | ...el sosten...<br>el soos-TEN |
| ...your shoes... | ...los zapatos...<br>los sah-PAHtos |
| Do not take off our underwear. | No se quite la ropa interior.<br>noh seh KEEteh...lah ROH-pah een-TEHReeor |
| Take off everything except your underwear. | Quítese todo la ropa excepto la ropa interior.<br>KEEteh-seh TOH-doh lah ROH-pah ek-SEPtoh lah ROH-pah een-TEHReeor |
| Come out when you are ready. | Salga cuando está listo.<br>SAL-gah KWAN-doh es-TAH LEES-toh |
| Go to... | Vaya...<br>BAH-jah |
| ...room 1. | ...al cuarto número uno.<br>al KWAR-toh NOOmeh-roh oonoh |
| ...the waiting room. | ...a la sala de espera.<br>...ah lah SAL-ah deh es-PEHrah |
| The bathroom is occupied. | El cuarto de baño está ocupado.<br>el KWAR-toh deh BAH-nyoh es-TAH oh-koo-PAHdoh |

# ULTRASOUND/ RECUMBENT EXAMINATIONS

| | |
|---|---|
| Is your bladder full? | ¿Es la vesícula llena?<br>Es lah beh-SEEcoo-lah JEH-nah |
| How much water did you drink? | ¿Cuánta agua tomó usted?<br>QWAN-tah AH-gwah toh-MOH oosTED |
| Did you drink the water? | ¿Tomó el agua?<br>tohMOH el AHgwah |
| Use this (point) to get on the table. | Use esto para subir a la mesa.<br>OOseh ES-toh PAH-rah soo-BEER AH LAH MEH-sah |
| Use the step-on stool. | Use el escalón.<br>OOseh el es-kah-LON |
| Can you move over onto the bed? | ¿Puede moverse hacia la cama?<br>PWEH-deh moh-VERseh AHsee-ah lah KAH-mah |
| Be careful. | Cuidado/ Tengo cuidado.<br>kwee-DAHdoh / TEHN-goh kwee-DAHdoh |
| Watch your head. | Cuidado con la cabeza.<br>kwee-DAHdoh con lah kah-BEHsah |
| Climb up... | Súbase...<br>SOObah-seh |
| ...on the table. | ...en la mesa.<br>...en lah MEH-sah |
| Lie down. | Acuéstese.<br>ah-KOOESteh-seh |
| Lie on... | Acuéstese...<br>ah-KOOESteh-seh... |
| ...your back. | ...en la espalda.<br>en lah es-PALdah |

## Spanish for Radiology Professionals

| | |
|---|---|
| ...your left/right side. | ...en el lado izquierda /derecha.<br>en el LAH-doh ees-KEYEERdah /deh-REHchah |
| ...your stomach. | ...en el estómago.<br>en el es-TOHmah-goh |
| ...the table. | ...en la mesa.<br>en lah MEH-sah |
| Stay in the center of the table. | Quédese en el centro de la mesa.<br>KEHdeh-seh en el SEN-troh deh lah MEH-sah |
| Move to your left/right. | Más para la izquierda/derecha.<br>mas PAH-rah lah ees-KEYEERdah/deh-REHchah |
| Move closer to me. | Más cerca de mi.<br>mas SER-kah deh mee |
| Put your feet at this end of the table. | Coloque los pies a este final de la mesa.<br>koh-LOHkeh los PEE-es ah ES-teh fee-NAL deh lah MEH-sah |
| Keep your hands above your head. | Mantenga las manos sobre la cabeza.<br>man-TENgah las MAH-nos SOH-breh lah kah-BEHsah |
| Put your hands... | Coloca las manos...<br>koh-LOHkah las MAH-nos |
| ...above your head. | ...sobre la cabeza.<br>SOH-breh lah cah-BEHsah |
| ...by your side. | ...a el lado.<br>ah el LAH-doh |
| Turn on... | Colóquese...<br>koh-LOHkeh-seh |
| ...your back. | ...boca arriba.<br>BOH-kah ah-REEbah |

| | |
|---|---|
| ...your side(right/left). | ...el lado(derecho/izquierdo).<br>el LAH-doh (deh-REHchoh/ ees-KEYEERdoh |
| ...your stomach. | ...boca abojo.<br>BOH-kah ah-BAHoh |
| Turn.. | Muévase...<br>MOO-EHbah-seh |
| ...to me. | ...hacia mi.<br>AH-seeah mee |
| ...away from me. | ...lejos de mi.<br>LEH-hos deh mee |
| Turn over. | Voltéese.<br>bol-TEHeh-seh |

# ERECT EXAMINATIONS

| | |
|---|---|
| Can you stand for a few minutes only? | ¿Se puede parar de pie por solo unos minutos? <br> seh PWEH-deh pah-RAR deh PEE-eh pohr SOH-loh OOnos mee-NOOtos |
| Can you... | ¿Puede usted... <br> PWEH-deh oosTED |
| ...stand up? | ...pararse? <br> pahRAHR-seh |
| ...sit down? | ...siéntese? <br> seeEN-teh-seh |
| ...lie down? | ...acuéstese? <br> ah-KOOESteh-seh |
| ...lift/raise your hand? | ...levantar la mano? <br> ...leh-banTAR las MAH-nos |
| ...move your head? | ...mover la cabeza? <br> moh-BER lah kah-BEHsah |
| Stand here. | Párese aqui. <br> PAHreh-seh ah-KEE |
| Please stand upright. | por favor ponerse de pie /Párese derecho. <br> pohr fah-BOHR pohNERseh deh PEEeh PAHreh-seh deh-REHchoh |
| Stand up. | Póngase de pie. <br> PONgah-seh deh PEE-eh |
| Hold here. | Aguanta aquí. <br> ah-GWANtah ah-KEE |
| Put your chin here. | Coloque la barbilla aquí. <br> koh-LOHkeh lah bar-BEEyah ah-KEE |
| Bend ( or lean ) forward. | Recuéstese... hacia el frente. <br> -OR- hacia adelante <br> reh-KWESteh-seh AH-seeah el FREN-teh/ AH-seeah ah-deh-LANteh |

*Spanish for Radiology Professionals*

| | |
|---|---|
| Bend ( or lean ) backward. | Recuéstese hacia atrás.<br>reh-KWESteh-seh AH-seeah ah-TRAS |
| Step back. | Échese para atrás.<br>EHcheh-seh PAH-rah ah-TRAS |
| Step forward. | Échese para delante.<br>EHcheh-seh PAH-rah deh-LANteh |
| Step away... | Mantenga...<br>man-TENgah... |
| ...from the machine | ...lejos de la máquina<br>leh-hos deh lah MAHkee-nah |
| Sit...please. | Siéntese...por favor.<br>seeEN-teh-seh..pohr fah-BOHR |
| ...here... | ...aquí...<br>ah-KEE |
| ...on the table... | ...en la mesa...<br>en lah MEH-sah |
| ...on this chair... | ...en la silla...<br>en lah SEE-jah |
| ...over here... | ...aquí...<br>ah-KEE |
| ...over there... | ...allá...<br>...ah-JAH |
| Do not move | No se mueva<br>noh seh mooEH-bah |
| Do not move once I have positioned you. | No se mueva una vez que yo lo ponga en posición.<br>noh seh MOOEH-bah oona bes keh joh loh PON-gah en poh-see-SEEON |
| Please put your hand here | Coloque ,OR, ponga la mano aquí, por favor.<br>koh-LOHkeh/PON-gah lah MAH-noh ah-KEE, pohr fab-BOHR |
| Put your hands... | Coloque las manos...<br>koh-LOHkeh las MAH-nos... |

## *Spanish for Radiology Professionals*     87

...above your head
...encima de la cabeza.
...en-SEEmah deh lah kah-BEHsah

...by your side
...por el lado.
pohr el LAH-doh

Keep your hands away from...
mantener las manos lejos de su estómago...
mahn-TEHnehr las MAH-nos LEH-hos

...your chest.
... de su pecho.
deh soo PEH-choh

...your stomach.
...de su estómago.
deh soo es-TOHmah-goh

Keep your hands together
Mantenga las manos juntas/os    *
man-TENgah las MAH-nos HOON-tas/os

Take your hand off.
Quítese su manos.
KEEteh-seh soo MAH-noh

Lift both hands.
Levante ambas manos.
leh-BANteh AM-bas MAH-nos

Do not hold here.
No aguante aquí.
noh ah-GWANteh ah-KEE

Please hold... here.
Por favor aguantate...aquí.
pohr fah-BOHR ah-gwan-TAHteh...ah-KEE

...this bar.
...esta barra.
ES-tah BAHR-rah

Hold here...
Aguanta aquí...
ah-GWANtah ah-KEE

...with both hands.
...con ambas manos.
con AM-bas MAH-nos

...with your right hand.
...con la mano derecha.
con lah MAH-noh deh-REHchah

...with your left hand.
...con la mano izquierda.
con lah MAH-noh ees-KEYEER-dah

| | |
|---|---|
| Bend your elbow. | Dobla el codo.<br>DOH-blah el KOH-doh |
| Bend at your waist only. | Doble a la cintura solamente<br>DOH-bleh ah lah seen-TOOrah soh-lah-MENteh |
| Sit up. (to someone slouching) | Incorpórese -or- siéntese.<br>hacia delante<br>een-kor-POHreh-seh / seeEN-teh-seh<br>AH-seeah deh-LANteh |
| Sit back.(or move back). | Siéntese para hacia atrás.<br>seeEN-teh-seh PAH-rah AH-seeah ah-TRAS |
| Move your shoulder forwards. | Mueva el hombro hacia el frente.<br>mooEH-bah el OHM-broh ah-SEEah el FREN-teh |
| Please move back a step. | Por favor muévase para atrás.<br>pohr fah-BOHR mooeh-BAHseh PAH-rah AH-tras |
| Do not ...lean forwards. | No...eche hacia el frente.<br>noh ...EH-cheh ah-SEEah el FREN-teh |
| ...bend your knees. | ...doble las rodillas.<br>DOH-bleh las roh-DEEjas |
| Keep... your head up. | Mantenga...la cabeza arriba.<br>man-TENgah ...lah kah-BEHsah ah-REEbah |
| ...your hand down. | ...la mano abajo.<br>lah MAH-noh ah-BAHhoh |
| Turn your head... | Mueva la cabeza...<br>mooEH-bah lah kah-BEHsah... |
| ...to the left/right. | ...a la derecha/izquierda.<br>ah lah deh-REHchah/ees-KEYEERdah |
| ...away from the machine. | ...lejos de la máquina.<br>LEH-hos deh lah MAHkee-nah |

*Spanish for Radiology Professionals*

# OTHER NECESSARY INSTRUCTIONS

| | |
|---|---|
| Here is... | Aquí está...<br>ah-KEE es-TAH |
| ...a pillow. | ...la almohada.<br>lah al-moh-AHdah |
| Not like that. | No es como eso.<br>noh es KOH-moh ES-oh |
| Yes like that. | Sí es como eso.<br>see es KOH-moh ES-oh |
| No like this. | No como esto.<br>noh KOH-moh ES-toh |
| That's fine. | Eso está bien.<br>ES-oh es-TAH BEEen |
| O.K. | Está bien.<br>es-TAH BEEen |
| That's not right. | No está bien.<br>noh es-TAH BEEen |
| Step down. | Bájese.<br>BAHeh-seh |
| Step up. | Súbase.<br>SOObah-seh |
| Please wait for me here. | Espérame aquí, por favor.<br>es-PEHrah-meh ah-KEE, pohr fah-BOHR |
| Stay here. | Quédese aquí.<br>KEHdeh-seh ah-KEE |
| Wait here for a few minutes. | Espera aquí unos minutos.<br>es-PEHrah ah-KEE OOnos mee-NOOtos |
| Do not leave the room. | No deje el cuarto-or-No salga del cuarto.<br>noh DEHeh el KWAR-toh (noh SAL-gah del KWAR-toh) |

| | |
|---|---|
| I will be back in a few minutes. | Regreso en poco minutos.<br>reh-GREHsoh en POH-koh mee-NOOtos |
| Do not touch... | No toque...<br>noh TOH-keh... |
| ...here/there. | ...aquí/ allá.<br>ah-KEE/ah-JAH |
| ...anything. | ...alguna cosa.<br>ahl-GOONah KOH-sah |
| Keep the gown on. | Déjese la bata puesta.<br>DEHeh-seh lah BAH-tah PWES-tah |
| Put your clothes on. | Póngase la ropa.<br>PONgah-seh lah ROH-pah |
| Let me help you. | Dejeme ayudarle.<br>DEH-heh-meh ah-joo-DARleh |
| The study is over now. | El estudio terminó.<br>el es-TOOdee-oh ter-meeNOH |
| You can...leave now. | Usted puede ...irse ahora<br>oosTED PWEH-doh...EER-seh ah-OHrah |
| ...go. | ...irse.<br>EER-seh |
| ...put your clothes on | ...Pongase la ropa<br>POHNgah-seh lah ROH-pah |
| Someone will take you ... | Alguien lo lleva ...<br>AHL-giehn loh JEH-bah... |
| ...upstairs. | ...arriba.<br>ah-REEbah |
| ...to your room. | ...a su cuarto.<br>ah soo KWAR-toh |
| You will be taken to your room shortly. | Pronto lo suben a su cuarto.<br>PRON-toh loh SOO-ben ah soo KWAR-toh |

## POSSIBLE RESPONSES

| | |
|---|---|
| I have to go the bathroom. | Tengo que ir el cuarto de baño.<br>TEHN-goh keh eer el QWAR-toh deh BAH-nyoh |
| I have to empty my bladder. | Tengo que vaciar mi vejiga.<br>TEHN-goh keh bah-seeAHR mee behHEE-gah |
| I cannot drink any more. | Yo no puedo beber más.<br>yoh noh PWEH-doh BEH-behr mas |
| I need to go to the bathroom. | Tengo que ir al baño.<br>TEHN-goh keh eer ahl BAH-nyoh |
| I can't. | No puedo.<br>noh PWEH-doh |
| I have... | Tengo...<br>TENH-goh... |
| ...pain in my left/right shoulder. | ...dolor en el hombro izquierdo/derecho.<br>doh-LOR en el OHM-broh ees-KEYEERdoh/ deh-REHchoh |
| I cannot... | No puedo...<br>noh PWEH-doh |
| ...move. | moverme.<br>moh-BERmeh |
| ...stand. | ...pararme.<br>pah-RARmeh |
| ...sit down. | sentarme.<br>sen-TARmeh |
| ...walk. | ...caminar.<br>kah-mehNAR |

# PATIENT EVALUATION

## GENERAL

See Chapter on filling out forms.

| | |
|---|---|
| What is your ... | ¿Cuál es su... |
| | kwal es soo |
| | |
| ...age. | ...edad. |
| | eh-DAD |
| | |
| ...temperature? | ...temperatura? |
| | tem-pehrah-TOO-rah |
| | |
| ...weight? | ...peso? |
| | PEH-soh |
| | |
| ...height? | ...altura? |
| | al-TOOrah |
| | |
| Please can you... | ¿Por favor podría usted... |
| | pohr fah-BOHR poh-DREEah oosTED |
| | |
| ...write it down? | ...escríbalo? |
| | es-kree-BAHloh |
| | |
| ...speak more slowly? | ...hablar más lento? |
| | ab-LAR mas LEN-toh |
| | |
| On what date (day) did you have the accident? | ¿Cuándo qué el día accidente? |
| | KWAN-doh KEH el DEE-ah ahk-seeDEN- teh |
| | |
| Do you have a sore throat? | ¿Tiene dolor de garganta? |
| | tee-ENeh doh-LOHR deh gar-GANtah |
| | |
| Do you have... | ¿Tiene usted... |
| | tee-ENeh oos-TED |
| | |
| ...arthritis? | ...artritis? |
| | ahr-TREEtees |
| | |
| ...incontinence? | ...continencia? |
| | kon-tee-nenSEE-ah |

## Spanish for Radiology Professionals

| | |
|---|---|
| ...bood in your urine? | ...sangre en la orina?<br>SAHN-greh en lah oh-REEnah |
| ...chest pain? | ...dolor de pecho?<br>doh-LOHR deh PEH-choh |
| ...constipation? | ...constipación/estreñimiento?<br>kohns-tee-pahSEE-ON/ es-treh-nyee-MEE-ENtoh |
| ... a cough? | ...un catarro?<br>oon kah-TAHRrah |
| ...difficulty swalling? | ...dificultad tragando?<br>dee-fee-koolTAHD trah-GANdoh |
| ...frequency? | ...confrecuencia?<br>kon-frehKOO-ENsee-ah |
| ...goiter? | ...bocio?<br>boh-SEEoh |
| ...heart murmur? | ...ronquidos?<br>ron-KEEdos |
| ...high blood pressure? | ...presión sanguinea alta?<br>preh-SEEON san-GIHneh-ah AL-tah |
| ... any pain? | ...dolor?<br>doh-LOHR |
| ...sinusitis | ...sinositis?<br>see-nohSEE-tees |
| ...any swelling? | algún hinchazón?<br>ahl-GOON een-chahSOHN |
| How long have you had... | ¿Cuándo tiempo ha tenido...<br>QWAN-toh teeEM-poh ah teh-NEEdoh |
| ...the pain | ...el dolor?<br>el doh-LOHR |
| Are you... | ¿Es usted ...<br>es oosTED |
| ...anemic? | ...anémico/a?                              *<br>ah-NEHmee-koh |

| | |
|---|---|
| ... diabetic? | ...diabético/a?   *<br>dee-ah-BEHtee-koh |
| Do you have any... | ¿Tiene usted algún...<br>tee-ENeh oosTED ahl-GOON |
| ...anxiety attacks? | ...problema de ansiedad?<br>proh-BLEMah deh ahn-see-ehDAD |
| ...memory problems? | ...problema de memoria?<br>proh-BLEMah deh meh-MOHree-ah |
| ...trouble sleeping? | ...problema al dormir?<br>proh-BLEMah al dorMEER |
| Have you had any siezures? | ¿Ha tenido convulsiones?<br>ah tee-NEEdoh oosTED kohn-boolSEEOHnes |
| Do you have a history of ashma? | ¿Tiene historial de asma?<br>teeEN-eh ees-torREEal deh HAHS-mah |
| Do you know what test/study you are having? | ¿Sabe usted el estudio que tiene?<br>SAH-beh oosTED el es-TOOdee-oh keh teeEN-eh |
| Why are you having this study? | ¿Porque esta tomando este estudio?<br>POHR-keh es-TAH toh-MANdoh ES-teh es-TOOdee-oh |
| Was this study explained to you? | ¿Le explicaron el estudio?<br>leh ex-plee-KAHron el es-TOOdee-oh |
| What type of surgery did you have? | ¿Que operacion se ha hecho?<br>keh oh-peh-rah-SEEON seh ah EH-choh |
| Have you ever had any surgery or operations... | ¿Se ha operado algúna vez...<br>seh ah oh-peh-RAHdoh ahl-GOONah bes |
| ...on your stomach? | ...en el estómago?<br>en el es-TOHmah-goh |
| ...on your colon/intestines? | ...en el colon/intestino?<br>en el KOH-lon / een-tes-TEEnoh |
| Have you been vomiting? | ¿Ha estado usted vomitando?<br>ah esTAH-doh oosTED boh-eeTANdoh |

## *Spanish for Radiology Professionals*

| | |
|---|---|
| Have you had a... before? | ¿Ha tenido que tomar antes...? <br> ah teh-NEEdoh keh toh-MAR AN-tehs... |
| Have you been vomitting... | ¿Ha tenido vomito... <br> ah teh-NEEdoh BOHmee-toh |
| ...after meals? | ...despues de las comidas? <br> dehs-POOES deh las coh-MEEdas |
| Did you eat anything this morning? | ¿Comió usted algo esta mañana? <br> koh-MEEOH oosTED AHL-goh ES-tah mah-NYAHnah |
| Did you eat breakfast? | ¿Se desayunó? <br> seh deh-sah-jooNOH |
| Did you take an enema...? | ¿Se puso una enema...? <br> seh POO-soh oona ehNEH-mah |
| ...last night. | ...anoche. <br> ah-NOHcheh |
| ...this morning. | ...esta manana. <br> ES-tah mah-NYAHnah |
| ...yesterday. | ...ayer. <br> ah-JEHR |
| Do you have any pain...? | ¿Tiene dolor ...? <br> teeEN-eh doh-LOR |
| ... in your back. | ...en la espalda. <br> ...en lah es-PALdah |
| ...in your bladder. | ...en la vejiga. <br> en lah beh-HEEgah |
| Did you follow the prep instructions that you were given? | ¿Siguio usted las instrucciones para la preparacion que se le entrego? <br> seeGIH-OH oosTED las eens-trook-SEEOHnes PAH-rah lah preh-pah-rah-SEEON keh seh leh en-trehGOH |
| You are having an IVU... | Va a tener el estudio IVU... <br> bah ah tenEHR el es-TOOdeeoh IVU (ee beh OO) |

| | |
|---|---|
| ...today. | ...hoy.<br>oi |
| ...this morning. | ...en esta manana.<br>en ES-tah mah-NYAHnah |
| Have you had a barium meal before? | ¿Ha tenido que tomar antes bario?<br>ah teh-NEEdoh keh toh-MAR AN-tehs BAHree-oh |
| The doctor will give you something for the pain. | El médico le dará algo para el dolor.<br>el MEHdee-koh leh dahRAH AHL-goh PAHrah el doh-LOHR |
| The doctor will give the injection. | El doctor lo va a inyectar.<br>el dohk-TOHR loh bah ah een-jekTAHR |
| The doctor will put a plaster cast on. | El doctor le va a poner un yeso.<br>el dohk-TOHR leh vah ah poh-NER oon YEH-soh. |
| The doctor will see you. | El doctor lo verá.<br>el dohk-TOHR loh beh-RAH |
| The doctor will look at your leg... | El doctor le verá la pierna...<br>el dohk-TOHR leh beh-RAH lah PEE-ERnah |
| ...now. | ...ahora.<br>ah-OHrah |
| ...in a few minutes. | ...en unos minutos.<br>en OOnos meeNOOtos |
| The doctor will be conducting this test. | El doctor va a estar a cargo del estudio.<br>el dohk-TOHR bah ah es-TAR ah KAR-goh del es-TOOdee-oh |
| The doctor will be here... | El doctor estará aquí...<br>el dohk-TOHR es-tarRAH ah-KEE |
| ...in a little while. | ...en un momento<br>en oon moh-MENtoh |
| ...in ten minutes. | ...en diez minutos.<br>en dee-es mee-NOOtos |

## Spanish for Radiology Professionals

| | |
|---|---|
| ...soon. | ...pronto.<br>PRON-toh |
| Your leg is broken. | Su pierna está rota.<br>soo PEE-ERnah esTAH ROH-tah |
| You sprained your wrist. | Se dobló la muñeca.<br>seh dohb-LOH lah moo-NYEHkah |
| It's dislocated. | Está dislocado.<br>es-TAH dees-lohKAH-doh |
| The doctor wants you to have a x-ray taken. | Que el doctor quiera que usted se haga una radiografía/placa<br>keh el dohk-TOHR kee-EH-rah keh oosTED seh AH-gan OOnah rah-deeoh-grah-FEEah/PLAH-kahs |
| This wound must be stiched up. | La herida tiene que cosérse.<br>lah ehr-REEdah tee-ENeh keh kohSEHRseh |
| You will be admitted to the hospital. | Usted será admitido en el hospital.<br>oosTED sehRAH ad-meeTEEdoh en el ohs-peeTAL |
| You may need surgery. | Puede nesecitar cirugía/operación.<br>PWEHdeh neh-seh-seeTAR see-rooGEE-ah/oh-peh-rahSEE-ON |
| We must keep you here for a few hours. | Lo tenemos que mantener aquí por algunas horas.<br>loh teh-NEHmos keh mahn-tehNER ah-KEE pohr ahl-GOONahs OH-ahs |
| You will not be able to drive home after this exam. | (Usted) no podria manejar depues del estudio.<br>(oosted) noh poh-DREEah mah-nehJAR dehs-POOES del es-TOOdee-oh |
| You will not be able to drive after this test. | Usted no será capaz de conducir después de esta prueba.<br>(oosTED) noh sehRAH cahPAS deh cohn-dooSEER dehs-POOES deh EStah prooWEH-bah |

| | |
|---|---|
| Does your husband/wife know you are here? | ¿Su esposo/a sabe que está aquí?*that<br>soo es-POHsoh/sah SAH-beh keh esTAH ah-KEE |
| Would you like to call your home? | ¿Quiere llamar a su casa?<br>kee-EERreh jah-MAR ah soo KAH-sah |
| This is a consent form. | Éste es un consentimiento.<br>ES-teh es oon kon-sen-teeMEE-ENtoh |
| Please read this. | Por favor, lea esto.<br>pohr fah-BOHR, LEHah ES-toh |
| Please sign here. | Por favor, firme aquí.<br>pohr fah-BOHR, FEER-meh ah-KEE |
| Please sign this consent form. | Por favor, firme este consentimiento.<br>pohr fah-BOHR, FEER-meh ES-teh kon-sen-teeMEE-ENtoh |
| I need your consent for this study. | Necesito su consentimiento para este estudio.<br>neh-seh-SEEtoh suh con-sen-teeMEE-ENtoh PAH-rah ES-teh es-TOOdee-oh |
| I will get someone to explain this study to you. | (Yo) podría conseguir a alguien que le explique este estudio.    #<br>(joh) poh-DREEah kon-seh-GEER ah AHL-giehn keh leh ek-PLEEkeh ES-teh esTOO-deeoh |
| This is the consent form for this study. | Éste es el consentimiento para este estudio.<br>ES-teh es el kon-sen-teeMEE-ENtoh PAH-rah ES-teh es-TOOdee-oh |

\* Use -o- for the masculine and -a- for the feminine.

\# Pronouns in front of the verb can be omitted.

## POSSIBLE RESPONSES

| | |
|---|---|
| My temperature is 100 degrees. | Tengo cien grados de temperatura.<br>TEHN-goh SEE-en GRAH-dos deh tem-pehr-rahTOOrah |
| I've been vomiting. | He tenido vómitos.<br>eh tehNEEdoh BOHmee-tos |
| I am... | Estoy...<br>es-TOY |
| I've got... | Tengo...<br>TEHN-goh |
| My boood pressure is too high/low. | Mi presión sanguínea es demasiado alta/baja.<br>mee preh-SEE-ON san-GIHneh-ah es deh-mahSEE-AHdoh AH-ah/BAH-hah |

# FEMALE EVALUATION

Are you pregnant?

¿Está usted embarazada?
es-TAH oosTED em-bah-rah-SAHdah

At what age did your period begin?

¿A qué edad tuvo su primer period periodo menstrual?
ah KEH eh-DAD TOOboh soo preeMEHR pehr-REE-OHdoh mens-stroo-AL

What age did menopause begin?

¿A qué edad comenzó su menopausia?
ah KEH eDAD koh-mehnZOH soo meh-noh-PAUseeah

When was your last peroid?

¿Cuándo qué su último periodo menstrual?
QWAN-doh KEH soo OOLtee-moh pehr-REE-OHdoh mens-stroo-AL

Is your period regular?

¿Es su periodo menstrual regular?
es soo pehr-REE-OHdoh mens-stroo-AL reh-gooLAR

Do you have any spotting between periods?

¿Tiene algún sangrado entre períodos?
teeENeh ahl-GOON sahn-GRAHdoh ENtreh pehr-REE-OHdos

When was your last...

¿Cuándo qué su último ...
QWANdoh KEH soo OLtee-moh

...pelvic examination?

...exámen pélvico?
ekAH-men PEHLbee-koh

...pap test?

...prueba de cáncer en la cérvix?
prooWEH-bah deh KAHN-ser en lah SER-beek

Do you have any children?

¿Tiene a cualquier niño?
teeEN-eh ah qwal-KEEehr nee-NYOS

Have you had any pregnancies?

¿Ha estado usted embarazada alguna vez?
ah esTAHdoh oosTED em-bah-rah-SAHdah ahl-GOONah bes

...any still births?

...alguna nacido muerto?
ahl-GOONah nah-SEEdoh MWER-toh

| | |
|---|---|
| How many live births? | ¿Cuántos embarazos logrados?<br>QWAN-tos em-bah-RAHsos loh-GRAHdos |
| How old were you when you had your first child? | ¿Qué edad tenías cuando tuviste tu primer hijo?<br>KEH eh-DAD tehNEE-ahs QWANdoh tooBEESteh too preeMEHR EE-hoh |
| Have you had any abortions? | ¿Ha tenido algún aborto?<br>ah tehNEEdoh ahl-GOON ahBORtoh |

## POSSIBLE RESPONSE

| | |
|---|---|
| I have a vaginal infection | Tengo una infección vaginal.<br>TEHN-goh OOnah een-fek-SEE-ON bah-geeNAL |
| I am on the pill. | Tomo la píldora.<br>TOHmoh lah PEELdoh-rah |

# PREPARATION STUDIES

## GIVING AN INTRAVENOUS

The doctor will give the injection.
El doctor lo va a inyectar.
el dohk-TOHR loh bah ah een-jekTAHR

Please let us know if you feel sick...
Por favor, dejenos saber si se siente enfermo...
pohr fah-BOHR, deh-HEHnos sah-BEHR see seh seeEN-teh en-FEHRmoh

...after the injection.
...despues de la inyeccion.
dehs-POOES deh lah een-jek-SEEON

You may feel sick after you are injected.
Puede que se sienta enfermo despues de ser inyectado.
PWEH-doh keh seh seeEN-tah en-FEHRmoh dehs-POOES deh sehr een-jek-TAHdoh

Relax, the test will be over...
Tranquiliseze el estudio se terminara...
trahn-kee-LEEsee-seh el es-TOOdee-oh se ter-mee-nahRAH

...soon.
...pronto.
PRON-toh

...in half an hour.
...en media hora.
en meh-DEEah OH-rah

You will have to lie on this table...
Usted tendra que acostarse en esta mesa...
oosted TEHN-drah keh ah-kohs-TAHRseh en ES-tah MEH-sah

...for half an hour.
...media hora.
meh-DEEah OH-rah

...during the study.
...durante el estudio.
doo-RANteh el es-TOOdee-oh

Do not... sit up.
No se... siente.
noh seh...seeEN-teh

| | |
|---|---|
| ...lie down. | ...acueste.<br>ah-KOOESteh |
| ...turn on your side. | ...mueva de lado.<br>MOO-EHbah deh LAH-doh |
| Let me help you. | Dejeme ayudarle.<br>DEH-heh-meh ah-joo-DARleh |
| Please go to the bathroom and urinate. | Por favor vaya al bano y orine.<br>pohr fab-BOHR BAH-jah al BAH-nyoh ee oh-REEneh |
| Go to the bathroom, urinate then come back. | Vaya al bano, orine y luego regrese.<br>BAH-jah al BAN-nyoh, oh-REEneh ee looEH-goh reh-GREHseh |
| Please urinate then lie on your back on the table. | Por favor orine, luego acuestese boca arriba en la mesa.<br>pohr fah-BOHR oh-REEneh, looEH-goh ah-KOOESteh-seh BOH-kah ah-REEbah en lah MEH-sah |
| Please urinate now. | Por favor orine ahora.<br>pohr fah-BOHR oh-REEneh ah-OHrah |
| Please try again. | Por favor trate otra vez.<br>pohr fah-BOHR TRAH-teh OT-rah behs |
| Wait a few minutes and try again. | Espere unos minutos y trate otra vez<br>es-PEHreh OOnos mee-NOOtos ee TRAH-teh OT-rah behs |
| The toilet is this way. | El bano esta aqui.<br>el BAH-nyoh es-TAH ah-KEE |

# POSSIBLE RESPONSES

| | |
|---|---|
| I can't. | No puedo.<br>noh PWEH-doh |
| I tried but couldn't. | Yo trate pero no puedo.<br>joh trah-TEH PEH-roh noh PWEH-doh |
| I can't urinate. | No puedo orinar.<br>noh PWEH-doh oh-reeNAR |

# CONTRAST STUDIES

| | |
|---|---|
| Hold this (point) | Sostenga esto -OR- aguante esto   @<br>sohs-TENgah ES-toh/ ah-GWANteh ES-toh |
| Do not drink... | No beba...<br>noh BEHbah |
| Do not swallow... | No trague...<br>noh TRAH-geh |
| ...until we tell you to. | ...hasta le diremos.<br>AHS-tah leh dee-REHmos |
| ...until the doctor tells you to. | ...hasta el doctor le dira.<br>AHS-tah el dohk-TOHR leh dee-RAH |
| Drink the liquid...now. | Beber el líquido...ahora.<br>behBEHR el LEEkee-doh...ah-OHrah |
| Drink now. | Beber ahora.<br>BEHbehr-ahOHrah |
| Drink some more. | Beber un poco más.<br>BEHbehr oon POH-coh mas |
| Swallow some more. | Tragar un poco más.<br>TRAH-gahr oon POH-coh mas |
| Start drinking now. | Comience a beber ahora.<br>Koh-MEE-EHceh ah BEHbehr ah-OHrah |
| Stop drinking. | Deja de beber.<br>DEHhad deh toh-behBEHR |
| Drink... faster/slower. | Beba ... rápido / lento.<br>BEHbah... RAHpee-doh/LEN-toh |
| Take a little and hold it in your mouth. | Aguanta un poco en la boca.<br>ah-GWANtah oon POH-koh en lah BOH-kah |
| Take a big mouthful and hold it in your mouth. | Coje mucho y aguantalo en la boca.<br>KOH-heh MOO-choh ee ah-GWANtah-loh en lah BOH-kah |

## *Spanish for Radiology Professionals*

| | |
|---|---|
| Cough, please. | Tosa, por favor.<br>TOH-sah, pohr fah-BOHR |
| Put your hands... | Coloque las manos...<br>koh-LOHkeh las MAH-nos... |
| ...above your head. | ...encima de la cabeza<br>en-SEEmah deh lah kah-BEHsah |
| ...by your side. | ...por el lado.<br>pohr el LAH-doh |
| Take your hands away from... | Mantenga las manos lejos del...<br>man-TENgah las MAH-nos LEH-hos del... |
| ...your chest. | ...pecho.<br>PEH-choh |
| ...your stomach. | ...estomago.<br>es-TOHmah-goh |
| Turn on... | Coloquese..<br>koh-LOHkeh-seh... |
| ...your side.(right/left) | ...el lado. (derecho/izquierdo)<br>el LAH-doh (deh-REHchoh/ees KEYEERdoh |
| ...your back. (face up) | ...boca arriba.<br>BOH-kah ah-REEbah |
| ...your stomach. (face down) | ...boca abajo.<br>BOH-kah ah-BAHoh |

@ Either word is acceptable.

# POSSIBLE COMMENTS

| | |
|---|---|
| I cannot swallow. | No puedo tragar.<br>noh PWEH-doh trah-GAHR |
| I can't drink any more. | No puedo beber mas.<br>noh PWEH-doh beh-BEHR mas |
| I can't drink while lying down. | No puedo beber mientras estoy recostada.<br>noh PWEH-doh beh-BEHR meeEN-trahs es-TOYreh-kohs-TAHdah |

# ENEMAS

| | |
|---|---|
| I am going to insert a tube in your rectum. | Voy a colocar el tubo en el recto.<br>boy ah koh-lohCAR el TOOB-oh en el REK-toh |
| I am going to insert the tube now. | Voy a insertar o colocar el tubo ahora.<br>boy ah een-serTAHR oh koh-lohCAR el TOOB-oh ah-OHrah |
| The liquid is going in now. | El líquido esta entrando.<br>el LEEkee-doh es-TAH en-TRANdoh |
| Do not try to push the tube out. | No trate de pujar el tubo.<br>noh TRAH-teh deh poo-HAR el TOOB-oh |
| Do not try to evacuate. | No trate de evacuar.<br>noh TRAH-teh deh eh-bah-kooAR |
| Do not evacuate. | No evacue.<br>noh eh-bah-KOOeh |
| Please try to hold the barium/liquid in. | Por favor trate de retener el bario/líquido.<br>pohr fah-BOHR TRAH-teh deh reh-tehNEHR el BAHree-oh/LEEkee-doh |
| Please hold it in. | Aguante esto.<br>ah-GWANteh ES-toh |
| It will be uncomfortable. | Va hacer un poco incomodo.<br>bah ah-SEHR oon POH-koh een-KOHmoh-doh |
| The exam will last about... | El estudio toma alrededor de...<br>el es-TOOdee-oh TOH-mah al-reh-dehDOR deh... |
| ... ten minutes. | ... diez minutes.<br>dee-es mee-NOOtos |
| We will not put all of the barium/liquid in your colon. | No vamos a colocarle todo el bario/líquido en el colon.<br>noh BAH-mos ah koh-loh-CARleh TOH-doh el BAHree-oh/LEEkee-doh en el KOH-lon |

| | |
|---|---|
| We will be filling up your colon with the barium. | Nosotros llenaremos el colon de bario.<br>noh-SOHtros jeh-nah-REHmos el KOH-lon deh BAHree-oh |
| The barium is going in now. | El bario esta entrando.<br>el BAHree-oh es-TAH en-TRANdoh |
| The doctor will be monitoring this study. | El doctor estara a cargo de este estudio.<br>el dohk-TOHR es-tahRAH ah KAHR-goh deh ES-teh es-TOOdee-oh |
| Do not move. | No se mueva.<br>noh seh mooEH-bah |
| Only some of the barium will fill your colon. | Solo un poco de bario va a llenar el colon.<br>SOH-loh oon POH-koh deh BAHree-oh bah ah jeh-NAR el KOH-lon |
| I will allow you to go to the bathroom in a few minutes. | Yo lo dejare ir al bano en unos pocos minutos.<br>joh loh deh-harREH eer al BAH-nyoh en OOnos POH-kos mee-NOOtos |
| Please try to... | Por favor, trate...<br>pohr fah-BOHR, TRAH-teh... |
| ...relax. | ...de relajarse.<br>deh reh-lah-HARseh |
| ...to hold it in. | ...de aguantar o retener el bario.<br>deh ah-GWANtar oh reh-tehnNEHR el BAHree-oh |
| Breathe through your mouth. | Coja aire por la boca<br>KOH-hah AY-reh pohr lah BOH-kah |
| I am removing the tube now. | Estoy removiendo el tubo ahora.<br>es-TOY reh-mohBEE-ENdoh el TOOB-oh ah-OHrah |
| I will remove the tube in a few minutes. | Le quitare el tubo en unos minutos.<br>leh kee-tarREH el TOOB-oh en oonos mee-NOOtos |
| You can go to the bathroom.. | Usted puede ir al bano...<br>oosTED PWEH-deh eer al BAH-nyoh |

| | |
|---|---|
| ...now | ...ahora<br>...ah-OHrah |
| ...in a few minutes. | ...en pocos minutos.<br>en POH-kos mee-NOOtos |
| ...after I remove the tube. | ...despues que remueva el tubo.<br>dehs-POOES keh reh-mooEH-bah el TOOB-oh |
| You can evacuate the barium in the bathroom. | Usted puede evacuar el bario en el bano.<br>oosTED PWEH-deh eh-bah-kooAR el BAHree-oh en el BAH-nyoh |
| The barium is flowing back into the bag. | El bario esta bajando a la bolsa otra vez.<br>el BAHree-oh es-TAH bah-HANdoh ah lah BOHL-sah OT-rah bes |
| You can relax now, the test is almost over. | Se puede tranquilezar ahora, el estudio esta casi terminado.<br>seh PWEH-deh tran-kee-leh-SAR ah-OHrah, el es-TOOdee-oh es-TAH kah-SEE ter-mee-NAHdoh |
| The barium may make you constipated. | El bario te puede poner estrenido /constipado.   @<br>el BAHree-oh teh PWEH-deh ponEHR es-treh-NEEdoh /kon-stee-PAHdoh |
| You must drink plenty of liquids/water... | Usted debe beber mucho liquid...agua.<br>oosTED BEHbeh BEHbehr MOO-choh LEEkee-doh/AH-gwah |
| ...tomorrow. | ...manana.<br>mah-NYAH-nah |
| ...tonight. | ... esta noche.<br>ES-tah NOH-cheh |

@ Either word is acceptable

# POSSIBLE RESPONSES

I cannot hold it any longer.  
No puedo aguantar mas.  
noh PWEH-doh ah-GWANtar mas

I need to go to the bathroom.  
Necesito ir al bano.  
neh-seh-SEEtoh eer al BAH-nyoh

It is comming out.  
Esta saliendo.  
es-TAH sah-leeENdoh

Please stop!  
¡Por favor pare!  
pohr fah-BOHR PAH-reh

I don't feel well.  
No me siento bien.  
noh meh seeEN-toh beeEN

I will never be able to hold so much Barium inside of me.  
Yo nunca podre aguanta tanto bario dentro.  
joh NOON-kah POH-dreh ah-GWANtah TAN-toh BAHree-oh DEN-troh

# MAMMOGRAM EXAMS

## GENERAL QUESTIONS AND EXPRESSIONS

Are you pregnant?

¿Esta usted embarazada?
es-TAH oosTED em-bah-rah-SAHdah

Have you had x-rays of your breast before?

¿Ha tenido algun mamograma anteriormente?
ah teh-NEEdoh ahl-GOON mah-moh-GRAHmah an-teh-reeor-MENteh

...When?

... Cuando?
QWAN-doh

...Where?

... Donde?
DON-deh

Where were the x-rays taken?

¿En donde le tomaron los radiografias?
en DON-deh leh toh-mahRON los rah-deeoh-grah-FEEas

at...?

¿en...?
en...

...hospital/clinic/doctor's office.

...hospital/clinica/oficina de doctor.
ohs-peeTAL / clee-NEEkah / oh-fee-SEEnah deh dohk-TOHR

Please can you...?

Por favor podria usted...?
pohr fah-BOHR poh-DREEah oosTED

...write it down?

...escribalo?
es-cree-BAHloh

...speak more slowly?

...hablar mas lento?
ab-LAR mas LEN-toh

Is this a routine exam?

¿Es un estudio de rutina?
es oon es-TOOdee-oh deh roo-TEEnah

Is there something wrong...

¿Hay algo malo...
ahee AHL-goh MAH-loh

...with your breast?

...con el seno?
kon el SEN-noh

## *Spanish for Radiology Professionals*

| | |
|---|---|
| Why you are having this exam? | ¿Cuales la causa del estudio?<br>qwah-les lah KAH-OOsah del es-TOOdee-oh |
| Do you have pain in your breast? | ¿Tiene usted dolor en el seno?<br>teeEN-eh oosTED doh-LOR en el SEH-noh |
| ...a lump? | ...¿una masa?<br>oona MAH-sah |
| ...any nipple discharge? | ... ¿alguna secrecion por el pezon?<br>ahl-GOONah seh-kreh-SEEON pohr el peh-SOHN |
| How long have you had... | ¿Cuanto tiempo hatenido...<br>QWAN-toh teeEM-poh ah teh-NEEdoh |
| ...the pain? | ...el dolor?<br>el doh-LOR |
| ...the lump? | ...la masa?<br>lah MAH-sah |
| ...the discharge? | ...la secrecion?<br>lah seh-kreh-SEEON |
| This is a routine exam. | Este es un estudio de rutina.<br>ES-teh es oon es-TOOdee-oh deh roo-TEEnah |
| I will be taking two x-rays of each breast. | Voy a tomarle dos radiografias/placas de cada seno.    #<br>boy ah toh-MARleh dohs rah-deeoh-grah-FEEas/ PLAH-kas deh KAH-dah SEH-noh |
| I will have to compress your breast for this study. | Tengo que apretar el seno en este estudio.<br>TEHN-goh keh ah-prehTAR el SEH-noh en ES-teh es-TOOdee-oh |
| I an going to compress your breast. | Voy a apretarle el seno.<br>boy ah ah-preh-TARleh el SEH-noh |
| Have a seat. | Tome asiento -OR- Sientese.<br>TOH-meh ah-seeEN-toh seeEN-teh-seh |

| | |
|---|---|
| Stand here. | Parese aqui.<br>PAHreh-seh ah-KEE |
| Please hold... here. | Por favor aguantate...aqui.<br>pohr fah-BOHR ah-gwan-TAHteh...ah-KEE |
| ...this bar. | ...esta barra.<br>ES-tah BAHR-rah |
| Move your shoulder forwards. | Mueva el hombro hacia el frente.<br>mooEH-bah el OHM-broh ah-SEEah el FREN-teh |
| Do not hold here. | No aguante aqui.<br>noh ah-GWANteh ah-KEE |
| Please move back a step. | Por favor muevase para atras.<br>pohr fah-BOHR mooeh-BAHseh PAH-rah AH-tras |
| Step back. | Echese para atras.<br>EHcheh-seh PAH-rah AH-tras |
| Step forwards. | Echese para delante.<br>EHcheh-seh PAH-rah deh-LANteh |
| Step away... | Mantenga...<br>man-TENgah... |
| ...from the machine. | ...lejos de la maquina.<br>leh-hos deh lah MAHkee-nah |
| Take out your breast.<br>(from the machine) | Saque el seno.<br>SAH-keh el SEH-noh |
| Do not move. | No se mueva.<br>noh seh mooEH-bah |
| Lift your right/left arm. | Levanta el brazo derecho/ izquierdo.<br>leh-BANtah el BRAH-soh deh-REHchoh/ees-KEYEERdoh |
| Bend at your waist only. | Doble a la cintura solamente.<br>DOH-bleh ah lah seen-TOOrah soh-lah-MENteh |
| Do not ...lean forwards. | No...eche hacia el frente.<br>noh ...EH-cheh ah-SEEah el FREN-teh |

## *Spanish for Radiology Professionals*

| | |
|---|---|
| ...bend your knees. | ...doble las rodillas.<br>DOH-bleh las roh-DEEjas |
| Keep... your head up. | Mantenga...la cabeza arriba.<br>man-TENgah ...lah kah-BEHsah ah-REEbah |
| ...your hand down. | ...la mano abajo.<br>lah MAH-noh ah-BAHhoh |
| Turn your head ... | Mueva la cabeza...<br>mooEH-bah lah kah-BEHsah... |
| ...to the left/right. | ...a la derecha/izquierda.<br>ah lah deh-REHchah/ees-KEYEERdah |
| ...away from the machine. | ...lejos de la maquina.<br>LEH-hos deh lah MAHkee-nah |
| Come this way. | Venga aca.<br>BEN-gah ah-KAH |
| The study is over now. | El estudio termino.<br>el es-TOOdee-oh ter-meeNOH |
| You can...leave now. | Usted puede...irse ahora.<br>oosTED PWEH-doh...EER-seh ah-OHrah |
| ...go. | ...irse.<br>EER-seh |
| ...put your clothes on. | ...Pongase la ropa.<br>POHNgah-seh lah ROH-pah |

# The Spanish word, -placa- is commonly used to refer to an x-ray.

## POSSIBLE RESPONSES

No, I took it at...  
No, ya tomaron unas en...  
noh, jah toh-MAHron oonas en...

I have..  
Tengo...  
TEHN-goh...

...a lump.  
...una masa.  
oona MAH-sah

...pain in both breast.  
...dolor en ambos senos  
doh-LOR en AM-bos SEH-nos

...a nipple discharge.  
...secrecion por el pezon.  
seh-kreh-SEEON pohr el peh-SON

...pain in my left/right breast.  
Dolor en el seno izquierdo/derecho.  
doh-LOR en el SEH-noh ees-KEYEERdoh/ deh-REHchoh

I have had it for...  
Yo he tenido esto por...  
joh eh teh-NEEdoh ES-toh pohr

# MRI EXAMINATIONS

# GENERAL QUESTIONS

Have you ever had an injury to the eye involving metal?
¿Alguna vez has tenido una lesión en el ojo con el metal?
ahl-GOONah bes teh-NEEdo oona leh-seeOHN en el OH-hoh con el mehTAHL

Are you pregnant?
¿Está usted embarazada?
esTAH oosTED em-bah-rah-SAHdah

is there a possibility that you could be pregnant?
hay una posibilidad de que usted podría estar embarazada?
Ahee oosTED pohdREEah esTAHR em-bah-rahSAHdah

Are you breast feeding?
¿Es usted la lactancia?
Es oosTED lah lahk-tahn-SEEah

Do you have an history of cancer?
¿Tiene usted una historia de cáncer?
teeEN-eh oosTED oona ees-toh-REEah deh KAHN-sehr

Do you have sickle cell anemia?
¿Tiene anemia de células falciformes?
teeEN-eh ah-nehMEEah deh SEHloolas fah-see-FOHRmes

Do you have Wilson's disease?
¿Tiene la enfermedad de Wilson?
teeEN-eh lah ehn-fehrMEHdahd deh Wilson

Have you had a reaction to Gadolinium (MRI contrast)?
¿Ha tenido una reacción al Gadolinio (contraste de RM)?
hah tehNEEdoh oona reh-ahck-SEEoh al gah-doh-leeNEEoh (cohn-TRAHSteh deh ehreh ehmeh)

Do you have your previous MRI studies?
¿Tiene su precedente estudios de resonancia magnética?
teeEN-eh soo preh-sehDEHNteh ehs-tooDEEohs deh reh-sohn-nahnSEEah mahgNEHtee-kah

| | |
|---|---|
| Have you ever had an MRI study? | ¿Ha tenido alguna vez un estudio de RM?<br>hah tehNEEdoh ahl-GOONah bes oon ehs-tooDEEoh de ehreh ehmeh |
| Did you bring any previous MRI study with you today? | ¿Has traído estudio de RM anterior con usted hoy?<br>ahs trAH-REE-doh ehs-tooDEEoh deh ehreh ehmeh ahntehreeOHR kohn oosTED oi |
| Do you have any of the following? | ¿Tiene usted alguna de los siguientes?<br>teen-eh oosTED ahl-GOONah deh lohs see-GWEE-EH-tehs |
| Cardiac pacemaker. | Marcapasos cardiaco.<br>Mahr-kah-PAHSohs kahrDEE-AHkoh |
| Implanted cardiac defibrillator. | Desfibrilador cardiaco implantado.<br>dehs-fee-bree-lahDOR kahrDEE-AHkoh eem-plahnTAHdoh |
| Implanted neurostimulator. | Neurostimulator implantado.<br>neh-oo-roh-stee-moolahTOR eem-plahn-TAHdoh |
| Implanted drug infusion pump. | Bomba implantada de infusión de droga.<br>BOHMbah eem-planhnTAHdah deh een-foo-SEEohn deh DROHgah |
| Aneurysm clips. | clips de aneurisma.<br>KLEEeps deh ah-neh-oo-REESmah |
| Spinal stimulator device. | dispositivo estimulador espinal.<br>Dees-poh-seeTEEboh es-tee-mooLAHdohr es-peeNAL |

# *Spanish for Radiology Professionals*

| | |
|---|---|
| Penile implants. | Prótesis de pene.<br>PROHteh-see-ahs deh PEH-neh |
| IUD intrauterine device. | DIU dispositivo intrauterino.<br>deh-ee-oo dees-poh-seeTEEboh eentrah-ootehREEnoh |
| Heart valve prosthesis. | Prótesis de la válvula de corazón.<br>PROHteh-sees deh lah VAHvoo-lah deh koh-rahSON |
| Artificial limbs or joints. | extremidades o articulaciones artificiales.<br>ek-treh-mee-DAHdehs oh ar-tee-koo-lah-SEE-OHnes ar-tee-feeCEE-AHles |
| Tattooed eyeliner or eyebrows. | Delineador de ojos o cejas tatuadas.<br>deh-leh-NEH-AHdor deh OH-hos oh SEHhahs tah-TOO-AHdahs |
| Body piercing. (except ears) | La perforación del cuerpo. (excepto las orejas)<br>lah perh-foh-rah-seeON del KWEHpoh (ek-SEPtoh lahs ohREEhahs |
| Implants in the head. | Los implantes en la cabeza.<br>Los eemPLAHNtehs ehn lah cahBEH- sah |
| Shunt. | Shunt.<br>soont |
| Stent. | Stent.<br>Es-TEHNT |
| Harrington rods. | Barras de Harrington.<br>BAHR-rahs deh Harrington |

| | |
|---|---|
| Metal screws or plates. | Tornillos o placas metálicas.<br>tohrNEEyohs oh PLAHkahs mehTAHleekahs |
| Dentures. | Dentaduras.<br>dehn-tahDOOrahs |
| Wires, sutures or staples. | Alambres, suturas o grapas.<br>Ah-LAHMbrehs sooTOOrahs oh GRAHpahs |
| Shrapnel or bullets. | Metralla o balas.<br>meh-TRAHyah oh BAHlahs |
| Coils or filters. | Bobinas o filtros.<br>bohBEEnahs oh FEEL-trohs |
| Claustrophobia. | claustrofobia.<br>klahs-troh-FOHbee-ah |

# ADDRESSING THE PARENT/GUARDIAN

| | |
|---|---|
| Can you hold the baby while I take this test? | ¿Podria usted sostener el bebé mientras tomo este estudio? poh-DREEah oosTED sos-TEHner el beh-BEH meeEN-tras TOH-moh ES-teh es-TOOdee-oh |
| Hold the baby here. | Aguante el bebé aquí. ah-GWANteh el beh-BEH ah-KEE |
| Hold the baby like this (demonstrate) | Aquante el bebé de esta manera ah-GWANteh el beh-BEH deh es-TAH mah-NEHrah |
| Did anyone else come with you? | ¿Alguien más vino con usted? AHL-giehn mas BEE-noh kon oosTED |
| …a relative? | …un pariente? oon pah-reeENteh |
| …a friend? | … un amigo? oon ah-MEEgoh |
| Can your husband hold the baby? | ¿Puede tener su marido al bebé? PWED-deh tehn-NEHR soo mahREE-doh al beh-BEH |
| One of you will have to hold the baby during the test. | Uno de ustedes tendrá que sostener el bebe mientras yo toma el estudio. OOnoh deh oos-TEDes tehn-DRAH keh sos-TEHner el beh-BEH mee-ENtras joh TOH-mah el es-TOOdee-o |

| | |
|---|---|
| Is the baby cold? | ¿Es el bebé frío?<br>es el beh-BEH FREE-oh |
| Is the baby hungry? | ¿Está el bebé con hambre?<br>es-TAH el beh-BEH kon AHM-breh |
| Did you feed him/her this morning? | ¿Le dio de comer esta mañana?<br>leh deeoh deh coh-MER ES-tah mah-NYAHnah |
| Does the baby want... | ¿Quiere el bebé ...<br>kee-EHreh el beh-BEH |
| ...a pacifier? | ... un chupete/chupon/pacificador/ el bobo?  \*<br>oon chooPEHteh/chooPOHN/ pah-see-fee-CAH-dohr/BOH-boh |
| ..a bottle? | ... la botella/ el biberón?<br>lah boh-TEHyah/ el bee-behRON |
| ...a toy?   . | ...un juguete?<br>oon hoo-GEHteh |

\* Any of these words could be used.

# ENGLISH-SPANISH DICTIONARY

Words are listed in alphabetical order regardless of whether the entry is one or two words.

**Abbreviations:**

| | | | |
|---|---|---|---|
| conj. | conjunction | adj. | adjective |
| v. | regular verb | adv. | adverb |
| *v. | irregular conjugated verb | | |
| f. | feminine noun or adj | m. | masculine noun or adj |
| pl. | plural | sing. | singular |
| prep. | preposition | n. | numeral |
| pron. | pronoun | interr. | interrogative |

## A

| | |
|---|---|
| a | un; una |
| abdomen | abdomen,m. |
| able, be | poder,v* |
| abnormal | anormal,adj. |
| abort | abortar,v. |
| abortion | aborto,m. |
| about(place) | acerca de,prep. |
| above | sobre;encima de,prep. |
| above | arriba,adv. |
| abscess | abseso,m. |
| absent | ausente,adj. |
| absolutely | absolutamente,adv. |
| absorb | absorber,v* |
| abstain | abstenerse,v* |
| abusive | abusivo,adj. |
| accept | aceptar,v. |
| accident | accidente,m. |
| accompany | acompañar,v |
| account(bill) | cuenta,f. |
| accountant | contador/a, f/m |
| accurate | correcto,adj. |
| ache | dolor,m. |

| | |
|---|---|
| ache | doler,v*. |
| achieve | conseguir,v* |
| acid | acido,m. |
| acquire | obtener,v* |
| across | por,prep. |
| addict | adicto/a, m./f. |
| address | dirección,f. |
| adjust | ajustar,v. |
| administer | aplicar,v* |
| advise(counsel) | aconsejar,v. |
| advise(inform) | avisar,v. |
| afraid | miedoso,adj. |
| afraid(to be) | tener(v*) miedo |
| after(position) | detrás de,prep. |
| after(time) | después de,prep. |
| afternoon | tarde,f. |
| afterwards | después,adv. |
| again | otra vez,adv. |
| against | contra,prep. |
| age | edad,f. |
| agree | consentir,v* |
| ahead | delante; al frente,adv. |
| air | aire,m. |
| airport | aeropuerto,m |
| alcohol | alcohol,m. |
| all | todo,adj. |
| allergic | alérgico,adv. |
| allergy | alergia,f. |
| alone | solo,adj. |
| alone | solamente,adv. |
| along | al lado de,prep. |
| along with | junto con |
| also | tambien,adv. |
| always | siempre,adv. |
| almost | casi,adv. |
| among | entre,prep. |
| an | un;una |
| analgesic | analgésico,m. |

| | |
|---|---|
| anatomy | anatomía,f. |
| and | y,conj. |
| anemia | anemia,f. |
| anesthesia | anestesia,f. |
| anesthetic | anestésico,m./adj. |
| ankle | tobillo,m. |
| anorexia | anorexia,f. |
| another | otro,m.,adj.,pron. |
| anterior | anterior,adj. |
| antibiotic | antibiótico,m./adj. |
| anus | ano, m |
| any | alguno;algunos,adj./pron. |
| anybody | lguien;alguno,pron. |
| anything | alguna cosa,pron. |
| apart | aparte,adj. |
| apart | eparadamente,adv. |
| appointment | cita,f. |
| approximate | aproximado,adj. |
| apron | delantal,m. |
| architect | arquitecto/a, m/f |
| area | área,f. |
| arm | brazo,m. |
| arrive | llegar,v* |
| artery | arteria,f. |
| artificial | artificial,adj. |
| as | como; mientras; adv.,conj. & prep. |
| Ash Wednesday | Miércoles de ceniza |
| ask | preguntar,v. |
| ask a question | hacer(v*) una pregunta |
| asleep | dormido,adj. |
| aspirin | aspirina,f. |
| as soon as | tan pronto como |
| asthma | asma,f. |
| asthmatic | asmatico,adj. |
| at | a; en,prep. |
| athiest | ateo/a,m/f |
| August | agosto,m. |
| aunt | tia,f. |

| | |
|---|---|
| autopsy | autopsia,f. |
| autumn | otoño,m. |
| away | lejos,adv. |

## B

| | |
|---|---|
| baby | bebé,f./m. |
| back | espalda,f. |
| backbone | espinazo,m., |
| backwards | hacia atrás;para atrás, adv. |
| bag | cartera,f;bolso/a, m./f. |
| bakery | panadería,f |
| bandage | curita,f;venda,f. |
| bandaging | vendaje,f. |
| bank | banco,m |
| banker | banquero/a,m/f |
| Baptist | bautista,m/f |
| bar(rod) | barra,f. |
| bath | baño,m. |
| bathroom | cuarto de baño,m. |
| be(permanent) | ser,v* |
| be(temporary) | estar,v* |
| because | porque,conj. |
| because of | por |
| bed | cama,f. |
| bedpan | silleta,f;cómodo,f. |
| before | antes de; delante de; enfrente de, adv. |
| begin | comenzar, empezar,v*. |
| behave yourself | ¡portate bien! |
| behind | atrás,adv. |
| believe | creer,v*. |
| belly | vientre,m. |
| below | abajo;debajo, adv. |
| belt | correa,f;cinto,m. |
| bend | doblar(se), v |
| beneath | debajo de,prep. |
| beret | boina,f. |
| beside | cerca de, prep. |

| | |
|---|---|
| between | entre, prep. |
| Bible | biblia, f |
| big | grande, adj. |
| billing dept. | departamento de cobro, m. |
| birth | nacimiento, m. |
| birthday | cumpleaños, m |
| black | negro, adj. |
| bladder | vejiga, f. |
| blanket | mante, f. |
| bleed | sangrar, v. |
| blind | ciego, adj. |
| blood | sangre, f. |
| blood pressure | presión sanguínea, f. |
| blood transfusion | transfusión de sangre, f. |
| blood vessel | vaso sanguíneo, m. |
| blonde | rubio/a |
| blouse | blusa, f; camisa, f. |
| blue | azul, adj. |
| body | cuerpo, m. |
| bone | huesp, m. |
| book | libro, m. |
| bookstore | librería, f |
| boot | bota, f. |
| both | ambos, adj. & pron. |
| bottle(baby) | botella, f; biberon, m. |
| bottom | fondo, m. |
| bowels | intestino, mpl. |
| boy | niño, m; chico, m. |
| bracelet | brazalete, m. |
| brain | cerebro, m. |
| barrette | hebilla, f |
| brassiere | sostén, m. |
| breakfast | desyuno, m. |
| breast | seno, m. |
| breath | respiro, m. |
| breathe | respirar, v. |
| breathing | respiración, f. |
| bring | llevar, v |

| | |
|---|---|
| brother | hermano,m. |
| brown | moreno;café, adj. |
| brunette | moreno/a |
| Buddhist | budista,m/f |
| burn | quemadura,f. |
| burn | quemar,v |
| bus driver | conductor/a, m/f. |
| business | ocupación,f; trabajo,m. |
| businessman | el hombre de negocios,m |
| businesswoman | la mujer de negocios,f |
| busy | ocupado,adv. |
| but | pero, conj./prep./adv. |
| buttock | nalga,m. |
| button | botón,m. |
| by | por, prep. |
| by (near) | cerca de,adv. |

## C

| | |
|---|---|
| cafe | café, m. |
| cafeteria | restaurante,m. |
| call(only phone) | llamar(v*) por teléfono |
| calm | calma,f. |
| calm | calmar,v. |
| calm down | calmar(se), aquietarse,v. |
| cancel | cancelar,v. |
| cancer | cáncer,m. |
| candy | dulce,m.;bombón,m. |
| cane(for walking) | bastón,m. |
| cap | gorro,m. |
| capillary | capilar,adj. |
| car | coche,m.;auto,m. |
| card | tarjeta,f. |
| care | cuidado,m. |
| career | profesión,f. |
| careful(to be) | tener(v*) cuidado |
| carpenter | carpintero/a,m/f |
| carry | llevar,v. |
| cashier | cajero/a, m/f |

| | |
|---|---|
| cataract | catarata,f. |
| cause | causa,f. |
| Catholic | católico/a, m/f |
| cavity(tooth) | carie,f. |
| center | centro,m. |
| cervix | cerviz,f. |
| chain | cadena,f. |
| chair | silla,f. |
| chaplain | capellán, m |
| check(bank) | cheque,m. |
| checkbook | talonario de cheques,m |
| cheek | mejilla,f. |
| chest | pecho,m. |
| chewing gum | chicle,m;goma de mascar,f. |
| child | niño/a,m./f.;hijo/a, m./f. |
| childbirth | parto,m; alumbramiento,m. |
| chin | barba,f.;mentón,m. |
| chin(the point of) | barbilla,f. |
| choice | selección,f. |
|   to have no |     no tener(v*) otra |
|   other choice |     alternativa |
| choke | sofocar,v*. |
| Christian | cristiano/a |
| Christmas | Navidad, f |
| Christmas Eve | Nochebuena, f |
| church | iglesia,f |
| cigar | puro,m. |
| cigarette | cigarrillo,m. |
| city | ciudad,f. |
| clean | limpio,adj. |
| clear | claro,adj. |
| clergyman | clérigo,m.;pastor,m. |
| clinic | clínica,f |
| clock | reloj,m. |
| close | próximo,adj. |
| close(near) | proximo,adj. |
| cloth | tela,f. |
| clothes | ropa,f. |

| | |
|---|---|
| coffee | café, m. |
| coffee shop | tienda de café, m. |
| cold | frío, adj. |
| cold (illness) | catarro, m. |
| colic | cólico, m. |
| colon | colon, m. |
| color | color, m. |
| Columbus Day | día de la Raza, m |
| coma | coma, f. |
| comb | peine, m. |
| come | venir, v*; llegar, v*. |
| come back | regresar, v. |
| come down | bajar, v. |
| come in | entrar, v. |
| come out | salir, v*. |
| come off | soltarse, v*. |
| come up | subir, v. |
| comfortable | comfortable, adj. |
| compare | comparar, v. |
| complete | completo, adj. |
| complete | completar, v. |
| complexion | cutis, m. tez, f. |
| complicated | complicado, adj. |
| compress | apretar, v*; condensar, v. |
| computer | computadora, f. |
| concussion | concusión, f. |
| conference | consulta, f. |
| confuse | confundir, v. |
| confused | confuso, adj. |
| connect | conectar, v. |
| conscious | consciente, adj. |
| consent | consentimiento, m. |
| consent | consentir, v* |
| constipate | estreñir, v* |
| constipation | estreñimiento, m. |
| consult | consultar, v. |
| contact lens | lentes de contacto, mpl; letillas, fpl. |
| continue | continuar, v*. |

| | |
|---|---|
| continuous | continuo,adj. |
| cook | cocinera, m/f. |
| cooperation | cooperación,f. |
| copy | copia,f. |
| corduroy | pana,f. |
| corpse | cadaver,m. |
| correct | correcto,adj. |
| correct | corregir,v*. |
|   it is correct | está bien |
| correctly | correctamente,adv. |
| cotton | algodón,m. |
| cough | tos,f:catarro,m. |
| cough | toser,v. |
| court | corte,f |
| cousin | primo/a,m./f. |
| cranium | cráneo,m. |
| critical | crítico,adj. |
| crowd | pueblo,m. |
| cry | grito,m. |
| cry | gritar,v. |
| cup | taza,m. |
| cut | corte,m. |

## D

| | |
|---|---|
| dad | papá,m. |
| daily | diario,adj. |
| danger | peligro,m. |
| dangerous | peligroso,adj. |
| dark | obscuro,adj. |
| date | fecha,f. |
| daughter | hija,f. |
| day | día,f. |
| dead | muerto,adj. |
| deaf | sordo,adj. |
| death | muerte,f. |
| December | diciembre,m. |
| deep | profundo,adj. |
| dentist | dentista,f. |

| | |
|---|---|
| denture | dentadura postiza,f. |
| deodorant | desodorante,m. |
| department | departamento,m. |
| department store | centro comercial,m |
| devil | diablo, m |
| diagnose | diagnosticar,v* |
| diameter | diámetro,m |
| diaper | pañal,m. |
| diarrhea | diarrea,f. |
| die | morir(se), v*. |
| difficult | dificil,adj. |
| difficultly | dificultad,f. |
| digest | digerir,v* |
| digestion | digestión,f. |
| digestive tract | canal digestivo,m. |
| dilute | diluir,v*. |
| dim | obscuro,adj. |
| dinner | comida,f. |
| direction | dirección,f. |
| dirty | sucio,adj. |
| discharge | secretión,f. |
| disease | enfermedad,f. |
| disinfectant | desinfectante,m. |
| disinfectant | desinfectar,v. |
| distance | distancia,f |
| divorce | divorcio,m. |
| dizzy | mareado,adj. |
| do | hacer,v* |
| doctor | doctor/a,m/f; medico/a,m/f, |
| doll | muñeca,f. |
| dollar | dólar,m. |
| door | puerta,f. |
| doorknob | tirador de puerta, f. |
| dorsal spine | espina dorsal,f. |
| doorway | entrada,f. |
| douche | ducha vaginal,f. |
| down | abajo; hacia abajo,adv. |
| dress | vestidura,f. |

| | |
|---|---|
| dress | vestir(se),v*. |
| dressing(bandage) | bendage,m. |
| drink | beber,v. |
| drive (a car) | guiar,v* |
| drowsy | soñoliento, adj. |
| drug | droga,f. |
| drug addict | drogadicto,m. |
| drugstore | farmacia,f. |
| drunk(to get) | emborracharse,v. |
| dry | seco,adj. |
| dull pain dolor | sordo,m. |
| during | durante,prep. |

**E**

| | |
|---|---|
| each | cada,adj. |
| ear | oreja,f. |
| eardrum | tímpano, m |
| early | temprano,adj. |
| earrings | aretes,mpl; pendientes,mpl |
| easy | fácil,adj. |
| eat | comer,v. |
| eat breakfast | desayunarse,v; tomar(v.) el desaynno |
| eat diner | tomar(v.) la comida |
| edge | borde,m. |
| eight | ocho,n. |
| eighteen | dieciocho,n. |
| eighty | ochenta,n. |
| either | uno u otro,pron. |
| either of the two | cualquiera de los dos |
| elbow | codo,m. |
| elderly | viejo,adj. |
| elevator | ascensor,m; elevador,m. |
| eleven | once,n. |
| else | otro,adj. & adv. |
| elsewhere | en otro parte,adv. |
| emergency | emergencia,f. |
| emphysema | enfisema,f. |
| employee | empleado,m. |

| | |
|---|---|
| employer | patrón,m. |
| employment | ocupación,f. |
| empty | vacío,adj. |
| end | terminar,v. |
| enema | enema,f. |
| English | inglés,adj. |
| enough | bastante,adv. |
| enter | entrar,v. |
| entire | todo,adj. |
| entrance | entrada,f. |
| envelope | sobre,m. |
| epidemic | epidemia,f. |
| Episcopalian | anglicano/a; episcopalista,m/f |
| equal | igual,adj. |
| equipment | equipo,m. |
| evacuate | evacuar,v. |
| Evangelical | evangélico/a,m/f |
| evening | tarde,f. |
| ever | siempre,adv. |
| every | cada,adj. |
| every other day | cada dos días |
| everybody | todos;todo el mundo,pron. |
| everyday | cada día,adj. |
| everyone | todos; cada uno,pron. |
| everything | todo,pron. |
| everywhere | por; en, adv. |
| exact | exacto,adj. |
| examination | exámen,m; estudio,m. |
| examine | examinar,v. |
| except | excepto;menos,prep. |
| excess | exceso,m |
| excuse | excusa,f. |
| excuse | excusar,v. |
| exit | salida,f. |
| expect | aguarder,v. |
| expensive | costoso,adj. |
| expert | experto,m. |
| expire | expirar,v. |

| | |
|---|---|
| explain | explicar,v. |
| eye | ojo,m. |
| eyeball | globo del ojo,m. |
| eyebrow | ceja,f. |
| eyeglass | lente,m. |
| eyelash | pestaña,f. |
| eyelid | párpado,m. |
| eye sight | vista,f. |

**F**

| | |
|---|---|
| fabric | género,m. |
| face | cara,f. |
| facial tissue | papel facial,m. |
| Fahrenheit | Fahrenheit,adj |
| faint | débil,adj. |
| faint | desmayarse,v. |
| faint | desmayo,m. |
| faith | fe, f |
| fall | caída,f. |
| fall | caer,v*. |
| fall asleep | dormir(se),v*. |
| family | familia,f. |
| family name | apellido,m. |
| far | lejos,adj. |
| farmer | campesino/a,m/f |
| fast | rápido,adj |
| fasten | fijar,v. |
| fat | gordo,adj. |
| father | padre,m. |
| father-in-law | suegro,m. |
| Father's Day | día del Padre, m |
| faucet | grifo,m. |
| February | febrero,m. |
| feed | dar(v.*) de comer |
| feel | sentir,* |
| feet | pie,m. |
| female | hembra,f. |
| femur | fémur,m. |

| | |
|---|---|
| fetus | feto,m. |
| fever | fiebre,f. |
| feverish | febril,adj. |
| few | pocos,adj. |
| fiftee | quince,n. |
| fifty | cincuenta,n. |
| fight | lucha,f. |
| fight | lunchar,v. |
| fill | llenar,v. |
| final | final,adj. |
| find | encontrar,v*. |
| fine | perfecto,adj. |
| finger | dedo (de la mano),m. |
| fingernail | uña,f. |
| finish | fin,m;término,m. |
| finish | terminar,v. |
| fire | fuego,m. |
| fire station | estación de bomberos,f |
| first | primero,adj. |
| first aid | primeros auxilios,m.pl. |
| first floor | primer piso. |
| fist | puño,m. |
| five | cinco,n. |
| fix | remendar,v*;ajustar,v. |
| floor | piso,m;suelo,m. |
| flow | flujo,m. |
| flow | fluir,v*. |
| flu | gripe,f;influenza,f. |
| fluids | fluídos,m.pl. |
| fluctuate | fluctuar,v*. |
| fold(double over) | doblar,v. |
| follow | seguir,v* |
| food | comida,f. |
| foot | pie,m. |
| footstool | banquillo,m. |
| for | por;para,prep. |
| forearm | antebrazo,m. |
| forehead | frente,f. |

| | |
|---|---|
| forget | olvidar,v. |
| forgive | perdoner,v. |
| form | forma,f. |
| forty | cuarenta,n. |
| four | cuatro ,n. |
| fourteen | catorce,n. |
| forth | cuatro,n. |
| forward | hacia adelante;hacia el frente,adv. |
| free(no fee) | gratis,adj. |
| frequency | frecuencia,f |
| Friday | viernes,m. |
| friend | amigo,m. |
| from | de,prep. |
| front | frente,m. |
| front of | delante de |
| full | lleno;completo,adj. |

## G

| | |
|---|---|
| gallbladder | vesícula (biliar),f; vejiga de la hiel,f. |
| gallon | galón,m |
| gallstones | cálculo biliar,m. |
| gap | abertura,f. |
| gardener | jardinero/a,m/f |
| gargle | gárgarear,v. |
| gastric | gástrico,adj. |
| gastrointestinal | gastrointestinal,adj. |
| gas station | gasolinera,f |
| gate | entrada,f. |
| gauze | gasa,f. |
| gay | homosexual,adj. |
| gentle | suave,adj. |
| germ | germen microbío,m. |
| get | obtener,v* |
| get down | bajar,v. |
| get on | subir(v.) a |
| get out | salir,v* |
| get up | levantarse,v. |
| girl | niña,f. |

| | |
|---|---|
| give | dar,v* |
| glad | contento,adj. |
| glad(to be) | alegrarse(v.) de |
| gland | glándula.f. |
| glass(container) | vaso,m. |
| glass(for eye) | lentes,m;espejuelos,m. |
| glove | guante,m. |
| go | ir(se),v* |
| God | dios,m. |
| good | bueno/a,m/f |
| Good Friday | Viernes Santo, m |
| go out | salir,v* |
| goiter | bocio,m. |
| gold | oro,m. |
| good | bueno,adj. |
| good afternoon | buenos tardes |
| good day/morning | buenos días |
| good night | buenos noches |
| good bye | adios |
| gown(hospital's) | bata,f. |
| gram | gramo,m |
| grand child | nieto/a, m./f. |
| grand children | nietos,mpl. |
| granddaughter | nieta,f. |
| grandson | nieto,m. |
| grandfather | abuelo,m;papá grande,m. |
| grandmother | abuela,m;mamá grande,f. |
| green | verde,adj. |
| grey | gray,adj. |
| gum (glue) | goma,f. |
| gum (chewing) | chicle,m. |

## H

| | |
|---|---|
| hair | pelo,m. |
| hairbrush | cepillo para el cabello,m. |
| hairdresser's | peluquería,f |
| hair pin | gancho para el pelo,m. |
| half | medio/a,m/f |

| | |
|---|---|
| half hour | media hora,f. |
| hand | mano,f. |
| handbag | bolso/a, m./f. |
| handbag | cartera,f. |
| handful | puñado,m |
| handsome | guapo/a,m/f |
| Hanukkah | Hanukkah |
| hardly ever | casi nunca |
| hat | sombrero,m. |
| have | tener,v*;haber,v* |
| he | el,pron. |
| head | cabeza,f. |
| head ache | dolor de cabeza,m. |
| heal | curar,v;sanar,v. |
| health insurance | seguro médico,m. |
| hear | oír,v* |
| hearing aids | audífonos,mpl |
| heart | corazón,m. |
| heart murmur | ataque al corozón,m. |
| heart rate | velocidad del corazón,m. |
| heart trouble | enfermedad de corazón,m. |
| heat | calor,m. |
| heaven | cielo, m |
| heel | talón del pie,m. |
| height | altura,f. |
| help | ayuda,f. |
| hell | infierno,m |
| hemoglobin | hemoglobina,f. |
| hemorrhage | hemorragia,f. |
| hemorrhoids | hemorroides,f. |
| hepatitis | hepatitis,f. |
| here | aquí;acá,adv. |
| hereditary | hereditario,adj |
| high | alto,adj. |
| Hindu | hindú,m/f |
| hip | cadera,f. |
| hit | pegar,v. |
| hold | aguantar,v. |

| | |
|---|---|
| hold | tener(se),v*; sostener,v*. |
| hold on | agarrarse,v. |
| hold up | levantar,v. |
| holiday | día de fiesta,m;día festivo,m. |
| Halloween | noche de Brujas, f |
| home | casa,f. |
| homosexual | homosexual,adj. |
| hospital | hospital,m. |
| hour | hora,f. |
| how | cómo,adv./adj. |
| how | qué,interr. |
| how long | cuánto tiempo |
| how much/many | cuántos |
| how soon? | ¿cuándo? |
| hug | abrazar,v* |
| hundred | cien(to),n. |
| hunger | hambre,f. |
| hungry(to be) | tener(v*.) hambre |
| hurry | apresurar(se),v. |
| to be in a hurry | tener(v*) prisa |
| hurry up | presurar(se),v*;dar(se)(v*.) prisa |
| hurt | hacer(v*) año,dañar,v. |
| husband | marido,m.esposo,m. |

## I

| | |
|---|---|
| I | yo,pron. |
| ice | hielo,m. |
| ice chips | hielo,m. |
| identification | identificación,f. |
| if | si,adv. |
| ill | enfermo;malo,adj. |
| ill(to become) | enfermar,v. |
| image | imagen,f. |
| immediate | inmediato,adj. |
| immediately | inmediatamente,adv. |
| implant | implantar,v. |
| important | importante,adj. |
| in | en;dentro de,prep. |

| | |
|---|---|
| inch | pulgada,f |
| in front of | frente a |
| incision | incisión,f. |
| Independence Day | día de la Independencia,m |
| infant | bebé,m. |
| infect | infectar,v. |
| infected(to become) | infectarse,v. |
| infection | infección,f;contagio,m. |
| inflate | inflar,v. |
| influenza | gripe,f. |
| information | información,f. |
| inhale | inspirar,v. |
| inject | inyectar,v. |
| injected | inyectado |
| injection | inyección,f. |
| insane | insano,m.loco,m. |
| insert | insertar,v. |
| inside | dentro,adv./adj. |
| insist | insistir(v.) en |
| inspect | examinar,v. |
| instruct | instruir,v*. |
| instruction | instrucción,f. |
| insulin | insulina,f. |
| insurance | seguro,m. |
| insurance policy | póliza de seguro,f. |
| intelligent | inteligente,adj |
| intense | intenso,adj. |
| interpret | interpretar,v. |
| intestine | intestino,m. |
| into | en;dentro de,prep./adv. |
| intoxicate | intoxicar,v* |
| intravenous | intravenoso,adj. |
| invalid | inválido;enfermizo,adj. |
| iodine | yodo,m. |
| iris(of eyes) | iris,m; |
| I.V. | suero ó intravenosa,m. |

## J

| | |
|---|---|
| jacket | chaqueta,f. |
| jaw | quijada,f;mandíbula,f. |
| Jehovah's Witness | testigo/a de Jehová,m/f |
| jersey | jersey,f;blusa,f. |
| jewelry | prenda,f;joya,f. |
| Jewish | judío/a,m/f |
| job | trabajo,m;ocupación,f. |
| join | juntar,v. |
| joint | articulación,f. |
| Judaism | judaísmo, m |
| juice | jugo,m. |
| July | julio,m. |
| June | junio,m. |

## K

| | |
|---|---|
| keep | retener,v*. |
| key | llave,f. |
| keyring | llavero,m. |
| kidney | riñon,m. |
| kidney stones | cálculos,m. |
| kidney stones | piedra en el riñon,f. |
| kilogram | kilo,m |
| kilometer | kilómetro,m |
| kind | simpático/a,adj |
| knee | rodilla,f. |
| knife | cuchillo,m. |
| knock | golpear,v. |
| knock on the door | llamar(v.) a la puerta |
| knock kneed | patizambo,adj. |
| know(acquainted) | conocer,v* |
| know(knowledge) | saber,v*. |

## L

| | |
|---|---|
| labor(to be in) | estar(v*.) de parto |
| Labor Day | día del Trabajo, m |
| lady | señora,f;dama,f. |

| | |
|---|---|
| large | grande ,adj |
| laryngitis | laringitis,adj. |
| larynx | laringe,f. |
| last | último;final,adj. |
| last name | apellido,m. |
| last night | anoche |
| late | tardo,adj. |
| late(to be) | ser(v*.) tarde |
| lateral | lateral,adj. |
| lavatory | lavatorio,m. |
| lay | colocar,v*. |
| lawyer | abogado/a,m/f |
| lead | plomo,m. |
| learn | aprender,v. |
| least | menos,adj.pron. |
| leather | cuero,adj. |
| leave | dejar,v. |
| left | izquierdo,adj. |
| left(hand/side) | izquierda,f. |
| leg | pierna,f. |
| lens | lentes,mpl |
| Lent | Cuaresma,f |
| length | longitud,f |
| lesion | lesión,f. |
| less | menos,adv |
| let go | soltar,v*. |
| library | biblioteca,f |
| lie | acostarse,v* |
| lie back | recostarse,v; echarse(v.) hacia atrás |
| lift | levantar,v. |
| like | como,adv. |
| lip | labio,m. |
| lipstick | lápiz(m.) para los labios |
| liquid | líquido,m. |
| listen | escuchar,v |
| liter | litro,m |
| little | pequeño;poco,adj. |
| little finger | dedo meñique,m. |

| | |
|---|---|
| liver | hígado,m. |
| lobe | lóbulo,m. |
| locate | localizar,v*. |
| location | situación,f. |
| lock(door) | cerradura,f. |
| locker | armario,m. |
| long | largo,adj. |
| long ago | hace mucho tiempo |
|   how long it | cuánto tiempo |
|   is since | hace que |
| look | mirar,v. |
| look for | buscar,v*. |
| look into | examinar,v. |
| look up | levantar(v.) la vista |
| loose(slack) | suelto,adj. |
| loose(to come) | soltarse,v*. |
| lose consciousness | perder(v*.) el sentido |
| loosen | soltar,v*. |
| lose | perder,v*. |
| lubricant | lubricante,adj. |
| lubricate | lubricar,v*. |
| lubrication | lubricación,f. |
| lump | masa,f;bolsa,f. |
| lunch | almuerzo,m. |
| lunch(to have) | tomar(v.) almuerzo |
| lung | pulmón,m. |
| lymph | linfa,f. |

## M

| | |
|---|---|
| machine | máquina,f. |
| magnet | iman,m |
| magnetic | magnético,adj. |
| Magnetic Resonance Imaging | Resonancia magnética,f. |
| magnify | amplificar,v*. |
| maintain | mantener,v*. |
| make | hacer,v* |
| make-up | maquillaje,m |
| malignant | maligno,adj. |

## Spanish for Radiology Professionals

| | |
|---|---|
| malnutrition | desnutrición,f. |
| mama | mamá,f. |
| man | hombre,m. |
| man and wife | marido(m.) y mujer(f.) |
| manager | director,m: gerente,m/f |
| manner(way) | manera,f. |
| manslaughter | homicidio,m. |
| many | muchos,adj. |
| March | marzo,m. |
| mark | marca,f. |
| mark | marcar,v* |
| married | casado,adj. |
| marry | casar,v. |
| mass (size) | masa,f. |
| mass (prayer) | misa, f |
| maternity | maternidad,f. |
| May | mayo,m. |
| maybe | quizás;tal vaz,adv. |
| maximum | máximo,m |
| me | me;mí,pron. |
| meal | comida,f. |
| measles | sarampión,m. |
| mechanic | mecánico/a,m/f |
| medical | médico,m. |
| medical insurance | seguro médico,m. |
| medication | medicacion,f. |
| medicine | medicina,f; medicamento,m. |
| medium | mediano/a |
| meet | encontrar(se),v*. |
| membrane | menbrana,f. |
| memory | memoria,f. |
| Memorial Day | día de Comemoración de los Caídos, m |
| menstruation | menstruo,m; menstruación,f. |
| mental | mental,adj. |
| metabolism | metabolismo,m. |
| metal | metal,m. |
| metallic | metálico,adj. |
| meter | metro,m |

| | |
|---|---|
| Methodist | metodista,m/f |
| microscope | microscopio,m. |
| midday | mediodía,m. |
| middle | medio,m. |
| middle finger | dedo del corazón,m. |
| mile | milla,f |
| milk | leche,f. |
| milligram | miligramo,m |
| milliliter | mililitro,m |
| millimeter | milímetro,m |
| million | millón,n. |
| mine | mío,pron. |
| minimum | mínimo,m |
| minister | ministro,m;pastor,m. |
| minor | menor de edad,adj. |
| minute | minuto,m. |
| miscarriage | aborto,m;malparto,m. |
| Miss | señorita,f. |
| mistake | error,m. |
| mistake | equívoco,adj. |
| mistaken | equivocado,adj. |
| mix | mezclar(se),v*. |
| mixture | equívoco,m. |
| Monday | lunes,m. |
| money | dinero,m. |
| month | mes,m. |
| more | más,adj. |
| Mormon | mormón/a,m/f |
| morning | mañana,f. |
| morphine | morfina,f. |
| most | casi,adv. |
| mother | madre,f. |
| Mother's Day | día de la Madre, m |
| mouth | boca,f. |
| move | mover(se),v* |
| movie theater | cine,m |
| Mr. | señor,m. |
| much | mucho,adj. |

| | |
|---|---|
| mucous | mucoso,adj. |
| mucous membrane | membrana mucosa,f. |
| mumps | paperas,fpl. |
| murmur | murmullo,m. |
| muscle | músculo,m. |
| museum | museo,m |
| Muslim | musulmán/a,m/f |
| my | mi |

## N

| | |
|---|---|
| naked | desnudo,.adj. |
| name | nombre,m. |
| nasal | nasal,adj. |
| nausea | náusea,f. |
| navel | ombligo,m. |
| near | cerca,adv. |
| neck | nuca,f. |
| necklace | collar,m. |
| necktie | corbata,f. |
| nerve | nervio,m. |
| nervous | nervioso,adj. |
| nervous breakdown | crisis nerviosa,f. |
| neurotic | neurótico,m. |
| never | nunca; jamas,adv. |
| never mind | no importa |
| newspaper | periódico,m. |
| New Year's Day | día de Año Nuevo, m |
| New Year's Eve | Nochevieja, f |
| New Year's Eve | Fin de Año, m |
| next | próximo,m. |
| next to | junto a;al lado;después de |
| niece | sobrina,f. |
| night | noche,f. |
| nine | nueve,n. |
| nineteen | diecinueve,n. |
| ninety | noventa,n. |
| nipple | pezón,m. |
| no | no,adv. |

| | |
|---|---|
| nobody | nadie;ninguno,pron. |
| nobody else | ningun otro |
| nod | inclinar(v.) la cabeza |
| noise | ruido,m. |
| none | ningumo;nada,pron./adj. |
| noon | mediodía,m. |
| nor | ni...ni,conj./adv. |
| normal | normal,adj. |
| nose | nariz,f. |
| nostrils | ventanas de la nariz,fpl. |
| not | no,adv. |
| note | nota,f.apunte,m. |
| nothing | nada,pron. |
| nothing else | nada más |
| November | noviembre,m. |
| now | ahora,adv. |
| nuclear | nuclear,adj. |
| numb | entumecido,adj. |
| number | número,m. |
| nun | monja,f. |
| nurse | enfermero/a,m/f. |

## O

| | |
|---|---|
| obese | obeso/a,m,f |
| obey | obedecer,v*. |
| o'clock | de |
| occupation | ocupación,f. |
| October | octubre,m. |
| of | de,prep. |
| off(distance) | lejos,adv. |
| off(not attached) | suelto,adv. |
| office | oficina,f. |
| often | muchas veces,adv. |
| O.K. | bueno,adj. |
| old | viejo,m. |
| olfactory | olfatorio,adj. |
| on | en;a;sobre;encima de,prep. |
| once | una vez,adv. |

| | |
|---|---|
| one | un;uno,adj. |
| only | solo;solamente,adj. |
| onto | a;sobre,prep. |
| opaque | opaco,adj. |
| open | abrir,v*. |
| opening | abertura,f. |
| operate | operar,v. |
| operation | operación,f. |
| optic | óptico,adj. |
| optical | óptico,adj. |
| optician | óptico,m. |
| or | o;u(before -o- or -ho-) |
| oral | oral,adj. |
| orange | naranja,f. |
| orbit | órbita,f. |
| order(request) | order,m. |
| organ | órgano,m. |
| other | otro,m./adj |
| ounce | onza,f |
| outside | fuera de,prep; afuera,adv. |
| ovary | ovarío,m. |
| over | sobre;por encima de,prep. |
| overcoat | abrigo,m. |
| owe | deber,v;adeudar,v. |
| oxygen | oxígeno,m. |

## P

| | |
|---|---|
| pacemaker | marcapaso,m. |
| pacifier(baby) | bobo,m;chupete,m. |
| pain | dolor,m. |
| painful | doloroso,adj. |
| painkiller | analgésico,m. |
| painless | sin dolor;libre de dolor,adj. |
| painter | pintor/a,m/f |
| pajamas | pijama,f. |
| palate | paladar,m. |
| pale | pálido,m. |
| palpitate | palpitar,v. |

| | |
|---|---|
| pants | pantalón,m. |
| papa | papá,m. |
| paper | papel,m. |
| paper tissue | papel de seda,m. |
| paralysis | parálisis,f. |
| paralyze | paralizar,v*. |
| paramedic | parmédico/a,m/f. |
| pardon | perdón,m. |
| parent | padre,m;madre,f. |
| park | parque,m |
| partial | parcial,adj |
| Passover | Pascua de los hebreos, f |
| past | pasado,m. |
| pastor | pastor,m;clérigo,m. |
| pathology | patología,f. |
| patient | paciente,m;enfermo,m. |
| pay | pagar,v*. |
| pay attention | atender,v*. |
| payment | pago,m. |
| payment in full | pago total |
| pelvis | pelvis,f. |
| pen | pluma,f. |
| pencil | lápiz,m. |
| penis | pene,m. |
| penicillin | peninsulína,f. |
| people | gente,f. |
| percent | por ciento,m; porcentaje,m |
| period(menstrual) | periodo,m. |
| pH | pH,m |
| phalanx | falanje,f. |
| pharmacist | farmacéutico,adj. |
| pharmacy | farmacia,f. |
| pharynx | faringe,f. |
| phone | teléfono,m. |
| photo | fotografía,f; photographic |
| plate | placa,f. |
| picture | fotografía,f. |
| pill | pildora,f. |

| | |
|---|---|
| pillow | almohada,f. |
| pillowcase | prenda de almohada,f. |
| pin(safety pin) | imperdible,m. |
| pint | pinta,f |
| plasma | plasma,m. |
| plaster of Paris | yeso,m. |
| plastic | plástico,m. |
| please | agradar,v. |
| plumber | plomero/a,m/f. |
| pneumonia | pulmonía,f. |
| pocket | bolsillo,m. |
| pocket book | bolsa,f. |
| pocket knife | navaja,f. |
| point | punto,m. |
| poison | veneno,m;ponzoña,f. |
| police | policía,f./m. |
| policaman | policía,m. |
| polica woman | la mujer policía,m. |
| police station | policía, f. |
| poor | pobre,adj. |
| pope | papa, m |
| portable | portátil,adj. |
| pound | libra,f |
| **powder** | **polvo,m.** |
| pregnant | embarazada,adj. |
| preliminary | preliminar,adj./m. |
| prenatal | prenatal,adj. |
| preparation | preparación,f. |
| prescribe | prescriber,v*;recetar,v. |
| prescription | prescripción,f;receta,f. |
| pretty | bonito/a,adj |
| previous | anterior; anteriormente,adj. |
| priest | cura,m: sacerdote,m |
| prior | previo,m. |
| private | privado,m. |
| problem | problema,f. |
| proportional | proporcional,adj |
| prone | propenso,adj. |

| | |
|---|---|
| prostate | próstata,f. |
| Protestant | protestante,m/f |
| psychiatrist | siquiatra,f. |
| psychiatry | siquiatría,f. |
| psychologist | sicologo,m. |
| psychology | sicología,f. |
| public | público,adj./m. |
| pull | jalar,v. |
| pupil | pupila, f |
| purpose | ropósito,m;intención,f. |
| purse | monedero,m |
| pus | podre,f;pus,m. |
| pulse | pulso,m. |
| push | empujar,v;pujar,v. |
| put | poner,v*. |

## Q

| | |
|---|---|
| quantity | cantidad,f |
| quart | cuarto de galón,m |
| question | pregunta,f. |
| questionnaire | cuestionario,m;lista de preguntas,f. |
| quick | pronto;rápido,adj. |
| quiet | quieto,adj. |
| quiet(to be) | tapar(v.) la boca;callar,v. |

## R

| | |
|---|---|
| radiation | radioción,f. |
| radioactive | radiactivo,adj. |
| radiograph | radiografía,f. |
| radiology | radiología,f. |
| rape | violación,f. |
| rape | violar,v. |
| rapid | rápido,adj. |
| rash(on skin) | erupcíon,f. |
| ray | rayo,m. |
| reach | llegar,v*. |
| read | leer,v*. |
| reason | razón,f;causa,f. |

| | |
|---|---|
| receipt | recibo,m. |
| rectum | recto,m. |
| red | rojo,adj. |
| refund | reembolso,m. |
| refund | reembolsar,v. |
| refuse | rehusar,v. |
| regulate | regular,v. |
| reimburse | reembolsar,v. |
| related | relatado,adj. |
|   we are related | somos relacionados |
| relative | pariente,m./f. |
| relax | relajar,v; tranquilizar,v*. |
| release | soltar,v*. |
| remain | quedarse,v. |
| remove | quiter,v. |
| repair | reparar,v. |
| request | orden,f. |
| requisition | requisición,f. |
| respiration | respiración,f. |
| restaurant | restaurante, f |
| result | resulta,f;resultado,m. |
| return | regresar,v. |
| rheumatism | reumatismo,m. |
| rib | costilla,f. |
| right | derecho,adj. |
| right(hand/side) | derecha,f. |
| ring(for finger) | sortija,f. |
| ring finger | dedo anular,m. |
| roll | rollo,adj |
| roll over | dé la vuelta |
| room | cuarto,m; |
| room(large) | sala,f. |
| Rosh Hashanah | Rosh Hashanah |
| routine | rutina,adj. |
| rub (with alcohol) | fricción con alcohol,f. |

## S

| | |
|---|---|
| safe | seguro ,adj. |
| safety-pin | imperdible,m. |
| sag | combarse,v. |
| salesperson | el vendedor/a,m/f |
| saline | salino,adj. |
| saliva | saliva,f. |
| same | mismo;idéntico,adj. |
| sample | muestra,f. |
| sanitary | sanitario,adj. |
| sanitary napkins | toalla sanitaria,f. |
| Saturday | sábado,m. |
| say | decir,v*. |
| scale | escala,f. |
| scalp | cuero,m. |
| scar(on skin) | cicatríz,f. |
| scarf | bufanda,f;mantilla,f. |
| school | escuela,f. |
| scissors | tijeras,fpl. |
| scrotum | escroto, m |
| search | buscar,v* |
| second | segundo,adj. |
| secretary | secretario/a,m/f. |
| secrete | secretar,v. |
| secretion | secreción,f. |
| security | seguridad,f. |
| sedation | sedación,f. |
| sedative | sedativo,m; calmante,m. |
| see | ver,v*. |
| send | enviar,v*. |
| senile | senil,adj. |
| sensitive | sensitivo,adj. |
| separate | separado,adj. |
| September | septiembre,m. |
| seven | siete,n. |
| seventeen | diecisiete,n. |
| seventy | setenta,n. |
| sex | sexo,m. |

## Spanish for Radiology Professionals

| | |
|---|---|
| shake | menear(se),v. |
| sharp(pain) | intenso,adj. |
| shave | afeitar(se),v. |
| sheet | sábana,f. |
| shin | espinilla,f. |
| shirt | camisa,f. |
| shoe | zapato,m. |
| shoelace | gabete,m;lazo,m. |
| shop | tienda,f. |
| short (length of clothing) | corto,adj. |
| short(height) | bajo,adj. |
| shoulder | hombro,m. |
| shout | gritar,v. |
| shut | cerrar(se),v*. |
| sick | enfermo;malo,adj. |
| sickle | hoz,f. |
| side | lado,m. |
| signature | firma,f. |
| silk | seda,adj. |
| silver | plata,f. |
| since | desde que;depués (de) que,conj. |
| sinus | sinus,f;cavidad(en un hueso),f. |
| sinusitis | sinusítis,f. |
| sip | sorber,v;chupar,v. |
| sir | señor,m. |
| sister | hermana,f. |
| sit | sentar,v*. |
| sit down | sentarse,v*. |
| six | seis,n. |
| sixteen | dieciséis,n. |
| sixty | sesenta,n. |
| size | tamaño,m |
| skeleton | esqueleto,m. |
| skin | piel,f;: curtis,m. |
| skinny | flaco/a |
| skirt | falda,f. |
| skull | cráneo,m. |
| sleep | sueño,m. |

| | |
|---|---|
| sleep (to go to) | dormir(se),v* |
| slipper | zapatilla,f. |
| slow | lento,adj |
| slowly | despacio,adv. |
| small | pequeño,adj. |
| smaller | menor,adj. |
| smallpox | viruela,f. |
| smart | listo,adj. |
| smell | oler,v*. |
| smoke | fumar,v. |
| so | muy,adv. |
| soak | remojar,v. |
| soap | jabón,m. |
| social security | seguro social,m; seguridad,f. |
| sock | media,f. |
| socket(of eye) | cuenca del ojo,f. |
| soda | soda,f. |
| soft | tierno;dulce,adj. |
| sole of foot | planta del pie,f. |
| solid | sólido,adj./m. |
| solution | solución,f. |
| some | algún;algunos,adj. |
| someone | alguien;alguno,pron. |
| somebody | alguien,pron. |
| somebody else | algún otro |
| something | algo;alguna cosa,pron. |
| sometime | algún día;alguna vez,adv. |
| somewhere | en alguna parte,adv. |
| somewhere else | en alguna otra parte |
| so much | tanto |
| son | hijo,m. |
| soon | pronto,adv;presto,adv. |
|   as soon as | tan pronto como |
|   how soon? | ¿cuándo? |
| sore | dolorido,adv. |
|   to have a | attener(v*.) |
|   sore throat | mal de garganta |
| Spanish | español,m. |

| | |
|---|---|
| speak | hablar,v. |
| special | especial,adj. |
| specimen | espécimen,m. |
| speedy | rápido,adj. |
| sperm | esperma,f. |
| spill | verter,v*. |
| spinal | espinal,adj. |
| spine | espina,f. |
| spleen | bazo,m. |
| sponge | esponja,f. |
| spoon | cuchara,f. |
| spoonful | cucharada,f. |
| spouse | esposo,m. |
| square | cuadrado/a,m/f |
| squeeze | apretar,v*. |
| stair | escalón,m. |
| staircase | escalera,f. |
| stand | pararse,v. |
| stand aside | apartarse,v. |
| stand back of | colocarse(v*.) detras de |
| stand up | poner(v*.) de pie;poner(v*.) derecho |
| start | comenzar,v*. |
| starve | morir(se),v*. |
| starving | hambriento,adj. |
| State | Estado,m. |
| stay | quedar(se),v. |
| steam | vapor,m. |
| step(stairs) | pisada,f. |
| step aside | hacerse(v*.) a un lado |
| step down | bajar,v. |
| step out | salír,v. |
| step up | subír,v. |
| sterilize | esterilizar,v*. |
| stethoscope | estetoscopio,m. |
| still | quieto,adj. |
| still(to be) | aquietar,v;calmar,v. |
| stir | menear,v. |
| stomach | estómago,m. |

| | |
|---|---|
| stool(excrement) | excremento,m. |
| stool(furniture) | escalón,m. |
| stop | parar(se),v. |
| store | tienda,f. |
| straight | derecho;recto,adj. |
| strap(belt) | correa,f. |
| street | calle,f. |
| stretcher | camilla,f. |
| string | cuerda,f. |
| stroke | ataque,m. |
| strong | fuerte,adj. |
| student | estudiante,m./f. |
| study | estudio,m. |
| study | estudiar,v. |
| sue | demandar,v. |
| suffocation | asfixia,f;sofoco,m. |
| sugar | azúcar,f. |
| sulphate | sulfato,m. |
| summer | verano,m. |
| Sunday | domingo,m. |
| super | cena,f. |
| supermarket | supermercado,m |
| supervisor | superintendente,m. |
| support | mantener,v*. |
| sure | seguro,adj. |
| surface | superficie,f. |
| surgeon | cirujano,m. |
| surgery | operación,f;cirujía,f. |
| surgical | quirúrgico,adj. |
| surname | apellido,m. |
| sutures | suturas,f.pl. |
| swallow | tragar,v*. |
| sweet | dulce,m. |
| swell | hinchar,v. |
| swollen | hindarse,v. |
| synthetic | sintético,adj. |
| syringe | jeringa,f. |

## T

| | |
|---|---|
| table | mesa,f. |
| tablespoon | cuchara,f. |
| tablespoonful | cucharada,f. |
| take | tomar,v. |
| take off | quitar,v. |
| take out | sacar,v*. |
| talk | hablar,v. |
| tall | alto,adj. |
| tampon | tampon,m. |
| tap(faucet) | llave,f. |
| tap(hit) | tocar,v*. |
| tape(adhesive) | tela adhesiva,f. |
| taste | gustar,v. |
| taxi | taxi,m. |
| taxi driver | chófer,f: chófer de taxi, f |
| tea | té,m. |
| teacher | maestro/a, m/f |
| tear duct | conducto lacrimal, m |
| teaspoon | ucharilla,f;cucharita,f. |
| teaspoonful | cucharadita,f. |
| technical | técnico,m. |
| technician | técnico,m. |
| technique | técnica,f./adj. |
| technologist | tecnólogo,m. |
| technology | tecnología,f. |
| telephone | teléfono,m. |
| tell | decir,v*. |
| temperature | temperatura,f. |
| temple (on face) | sien, f |
| temporary | temporero,adj. |
| ten | diez,n. |
| tender | delicado,adj. |
| tendon | tendón,m. |
| testicle | testículo,m. |
| tetanus | tétano,m. |
| than | que,conj. |
| thanks | gracias |

| | |
|---|---|
| that | ese;esa;aquel; aquella,adj. |
| that | ése;ésa;aquél; aquélla,pron. |
| so that | para que |
| that is enough | eso basta |
| therapist | terapeuta m/f |
| there | allí;allá;ahí,adv. |
| there is/are | hay |
| thermometer | termómetro,m. |
| thermostat | termóstato,m. |
| these | estos;estas,adj. |
| these | éstos;éstas,pron. |
| thick(not thin) | espeso,adj. |
| thin(slim) | delgado,adj. |
| thing | cosa,f. |
| think | pensar,v*. |
| thickness | espesor,m |
| third | tercero,adj. |
| thirst | sed,f. |
| thirsty | sediento,adj. |
| thirsty(to be) | tener(v*.) sed |
| thirteen | trece,n. |
| thirty | treinta,n. |
| this | este;esta;esto,adj. |
| this | éste;ésta;esto,pron. |
| Thanksgiving | día de Acción de Gracias, m |
| thoracic spine | espina dorsal,f. |
| thorax | tórax,m. |
| those | esos;esas;aquelos; aquellas,adj. |
| those | esos,ésas;aquélos; aquéllas,pron. |
| thousand | mil,n. |
| three | tres,n. |
| throat | garganta,f. |
| thumb | pulgar,m. |
| Thursday | jueves,m. |
| thyroid | tiroides,f. |
| tie(fasten) | atar,v*. |
| tight(squeeze) | apretado,adj. |
| till | hasta,adj. |

| | |
|---|---|
| till | hasta que,conj. |
| time | tiempo,m. |
| time(hour) | hora,f. |
| tip(point) | punta,f. |
| tired | cansado,adj. |
| tissue | tejido,m. |
| to | a;para;hasta,prep. |
| to (try) | tratar(v.) de |
| tobacco | tabaco,m. |
| today | hoy,adv. |
| toe | dedo del pie,m. |
| toenail | uña (del dedo del pie),f. |
| together | juntamente,adv. |
| toilet paper | papel deexcusado,m; papel higiénico |
| tomorrow | mañana,adv. |
| tongue | lengua,f. |
| tonight | esta noche;a la noche,adv. |
| tonsil | amígdala,f. |
| tonsillitis | amigdalitis,f. |
| too | también,adv. |
| too many | demasiados |
| too much | demasiado |
| tooth | diente,m. |
| toothache | dolor de muelas,m. |
| tooth brush | cepillode dientes,m. |
| tooth paste | pasta dentífrica,f. |
| top of | encima de;sobre. |
| touch | tocar,v*. |
| toupee | peluca,f. |
| towards | hacia,prep. |
| towel | toalla,f. |
| toxin | toxina,f. |
| toy | juguete,m. |
| trachea | tráquea,f. |
| traction | tracción,f. |
| tranquilizer | sedativo,m./adj. |
| tranquilize | tranquilizar,v*. |
| translate | traducir,v*. |

| | |
|---|---|
| translation | traducción,f. |
| translator | traductor,m. |
| transportation | transportación,f. |
| transport | transportar,v. |
| trauma | traumatismo,m. |
| travel | viajar,v. |
| tray | bandeja,f. |
| tremble | temblar,v*. |
| truck driver | camionero/a,m/f; conductor de camion,m |
| try | probar,v*. |
| try to | tratar(v.) de |
| tub(bath) | bañera,f. |
| tube | tubo,m. |
| tuberculosis | tuberculosis,f. |
| Tuesday | martes,m. |
| tumor | tumor,m. |
| tungsten | tungsteno,m. |
| turn | volver(se),v*. |
| tweezers | pinzas,f.pl. |
| twelve | doce,n. |
| twenty | veinte,n. |
| twice | dos veces,adv. |
| twin | gemelos,m.pl./adj. |
| two | dos,n. |
| type | escribir(v*.) a máquina |
| typhoid | tifoidea,f. |
| typhus | tifus,m. |

## U

| | |
|---|---|
| ugly | feo/a,adj/m/f |
| ulcer | úlcera,f. |
| umbilical cord | cordón umbilical,m. |
| umbrella | paraguas,m. |
| uncle | tío,m. |
| unconscious | inconsciente,adj. |
| under | bajo;debajo de,prep. |
| under clothes | ropa interior,f. |
| undershirt | camiseta,f. |

| | |
|---|---|
| understand | comprender,v. |
| underwear | ropa interior,f. |
| undress | desvestir(se),v*. |
| unemployed | desocupado,adj. |
| unemployment | desempleo,m. |
| unemployment compensation | compensación por desempleo,f. |
| unfasten | desabrochar,v. |
| uniform | uniforme,m. |
| union | unión,f. |
| union(labor) | sindicato,m. |
| university | universidad, f. |
| unless | a menos que,conj. |
| unmarried | soltero,adj. |
| unroll | desenrollar,v. |
| unsafe | peligroso,adj. |
| unsatisfactory | no satisfactorio,adj. |
| until | hasta;hasta que,prep. |
| untrue | falso,adj. |
| up | arriba,adv. |
| up to now | hasta ahora |
| upon | en;sobre;encima de,prep. |
| upper | superior,adj. |
| upright | derecto,adj. |
| upside down | al revés; de arriba abajo |
| upstairs | arriba;en el piso de arriba,adv. |
| urethra | uretra,f. |
| urgent | urgente,adj. |
| urinal | urinario,m. |
| urinate | orinar,v. |
| urine | orina,f.(orines,m.pl.) |
| use | usar,v. |
| uterus | útero,m. |
| uvula | galillo de la garganta,m;úvula,f. |

## V

| | |
|---|---|
| vacant | vacante,adj. |
| vaccine | vacuna,f |
| vaccination | vacuna,f. |

| | |
|---|---|
| vaccinate | vacunar,v. |
| vagina | vagina,f. |
| Valentine's Day | día de San Valentín, m |
| Valentine's Day | día de los Enamorados, m |
| valve | válvula,f. |
| vein | vena,f. |
| venereal | venéreo,adj. |
| vertebral column | columna vertebral,f. |
| very | muy,adv. |
| vessel | vasija,f. |
| via | por,prep. |
| virgin | virgen,f./adj. |
| vitamin | vitamina,f. |
| voltage | voltaje,m. |
| volume | volumen,m |
| volunteer | voluntario/a, m/f |
| vomit | vomitar,v. |
| vomit | vómito,m. |
| vulva | vulva,f. |

## W

| | |
|---|---|
| waist | cintura,f. |
| wait | esperar,v. |
| waiter | mesero/a,m/f |
| waiting room | sala de espara,f. |
| wake | despertar(se),v*. |
| wake up | despertar(se),v*. |
| walk | andar,v*;ir(v*.) a pie |
| wall | paréd,f. |
| wallet | cartera,f;monedero,m. |
| want | querer,v*. |
| warm | caliente;cálido ,adj. |
| warmth | calor,m. |
| wart | verruga,f. |
| wash | lavar,v. |
| watch(look) | mirar,v. |
| watch(wrist) | reloj de pulsera,m. |
| water | agua,f. |

| | |
|---|---|
| weak | débil,adj. |
| wear | llevar,v;usar,v. |
| wearing | cansado,adj. |
| wedding | boda, f |
| wedding anniversary | aniversario de bodas, m |
| Wednesday | miércoles,m. |
| week | semana,f. |
| weekday | día de trabajo,f. |
| weekend | fin de semana,m. |
| weight | peso,m. |
| well | bien,adv. |
| what | que,pron. |
| what | qué,interr. |
| when | cuando,adv./conj. |
| when | cuándo,interr. |
| whenever | cuando;siempre que,adv./conj. |
| where | donde,adv. |
| where | dónde,interr. |
| which | cúal;cúales,interr. |
| while | mientras,conj. |
| white | blanco,adj. |
| who | quien;quines;que,pron. |
| who | quíen;quínes;que,interr. |
| why | por qué,adv. |
| wide | ancho;amplio,adj. |
| widow | viuda,f. |
| widower | viudo,m. |
| width | ancho,m; anchura,f |
| wife | esposa,f. |
| wig | peluca,f. |
| window | ventana,f. |
| windpipe | garganta,f. |
| wipe | secar,v*. |
| within | dentro de,prep. |
| without | sin,prep. |
| woman | mujer,f. |
| womb | útero,m. |
| wool | lana,f. |

| | |
|---|---|
| work(effort) | trabajo,m. |
| work | trabajar,v. |
| work(employment) | empleo,m. |
| worse | peor; más malo,adj. |
| worst | peor,adv. |
| wound | herida,f. |
| wrap | enrollar,v. |
| wiggle | menear(se),v. |
| wrist | muñeca,f. |
| write | escribir,v*. |
| wrong | equivocado,adj. |

## X

| | |
|---|---|
| x-ray | radiografía,f; rayo equis,m. |
| x-ray room | sala de rayos equis,f. |
| x-ray technologist | tecnólogo de rayos X |

## Y

| | |
|---|---|
| yard | yarda,f |
| yawn | bostezo,m. |
| yawn | bostezar,v*. |
| year | año,m. |
| yellow | amarillo,adj. |
| yes | sí,adv. |
| yesterday | ayer,adv. |
| Yom Kippur | Yom Kipur |
| young | joven,adj. |
| younger | menor,adj. |
| young people | gente joven,f. |

## Z

| | |
|---|---|
| zero | cero,m. |
| zip-code | código postal,m; zona postal,f. |
| zipper | cremallera,f;zípper,m. |

Thank you for using

Spanish for Radiology Professionals:

An English/Spanish Pocket Guide

# Author's Bio

As an established educator, lecturer and writer, Olive gives seminars on mammography and other radiography-related topics at conferences throughout the United States and Canada and her articles appear regularly in radiological journals and newsmagazines. She writes regularly for Radiologic Technology - Journal of the American Society of Radiologic Technologist and she is an editor with Oncourse Learning, a source for online CE Credits.

In 2014, 2015 and 2016 Olive was selected by RAD-AID and ASRT Foundation to be a technologist fellow with Asha Jyoti Women's Health project in Chandigarh, India. This was the start of a new commitment. In 2017 Olive was appointed Associate Program Manager, RAD-AID India and is now an enthusiastic team member in support of Asha Jyoti and similar RAD-AID sponsored radiology services in developing countries.

When not writing, Olive is often occupied with her other addiction—reading. Olive loves to hear from her readers, and may be reached at www.opeart.com or by email: olive@opeart.com.

Made in United States
North Haven, CT
24 October 2022